McNary of Oregon

M^CNARY
OF OREGON
A POLITICAL BIOGRAPHY

BY STEVE NEAL

For Brian Booth,
a fellow aficionado of
Oregon history and
thanks for helping
the OHS sign up
Tom for Western Imprints

Best wishes,
Steve Neal
10-1-05

WESTERN IMPRINTS
The Press of the Oregon Historical Society

Frontis: Senator Charles L. McNary in 1940, Washington, D.C. (Author's collection)

Support for the production of *McNary of Oregon* was made possible by the Western Imprints Fund.

This volume was designed and produced by Western Imprints. The Press of the Oregon Historical Society.

Library of Congress Cataloging-in-Publication Data

Neal, Steve, 1949–
  McNary of Oregon.

   Bibliography: p.
   Includes index.
   1. McNary, Charles Linza, 1874–1944. 2. Legislators—United States—Biography. 3. United States. Congress. Senate—Biography. 4. Vice-Presidential candidates—United States—Biography. 5. United States—Politics and government—1901–1953. I. Title.
E748.M156N43   1985   973.91′092′4 [B]   85-13692
ISBN 0-87595-173-2

Printed in the United States of America.

For my parents,
Ernest and Ellen Neal,
and my grandmother,
Lula G. Williams

Books by Steve Neal

McNary of Oregon: A Political Biography (1985)

Dark Horse: A Biography of Wendell Willkie (1984)

The Eisenhowers: Reluctant Dynasty (1978)

Tom McCall: Maverick (with Tom McCall) (1977)

Contents

Author's Note

THIS IS A political biography of Charles Linza McNary, who was a major influence in American politics for a generation and Oregon's most prominent public figure in the first half of the twentieth century. I have been researching this book since 1965 when a search of library card catalogs indicated that there had not been a McNary biography. Since his leading contemporaries in the Senate were the subjects of multiple studies, it seemed to me that a McNary book was long overdue. In my hometown of Salem, the local airport, one of the high schools, a golf course, street, and even a real estate company bore his name, and yet few people remember much about the man except that he once had been the Republican nominee for vice president. It is hoped that this book will tell them a good bit more.

I could not have undertaken this project without the assistance of the senator's daughter, Charlotte McNary Limerick, who kindly made available her father's correspondence with his family, his scrapbooks, and other pertinent documents. The senator's niece, Martha Allen, was also enormously helpful in sharing materials from the family archives as was Carlton Savage, a McNary cousin and former State Department official. The late Margaret Marshall, McNary's niece, was generous in granting me several interviews and providing me access to family papers.

Except for material which was retained by the family and to which I have had access, the bulk of McNary's private papers are in the Manuscript Division of the Library of Congress, where I spent more than two years sifting through old files. I also consulted the much smaller but useful McNary collection at the University of Oregon, and several McNary letters at the Oregon Historical Society. The staffs of the Franklin D. Roosevelt library at Hyde Park, New York and Herbert Hoover library at West Branch, Iowa were helpful in pointing me to additional McNary materials. The Robert A. Taft, John D. M. Hamilton, and Harold Ickes Papers at the Library of Congress were also useful as were the Wendell L. Willkie papers in the Lilly Library at Indiana University. The *Oregonian, Oregon Journal, Chicago Tribune, New York Times*, and *Philadelphia Inquirer* reference libraries all made available their McNary files for this project.

In addition to the members of the senator's family who spoke with me about McNary's life, so did many others including Joseph Alsop, Ralph H. Cake, Henry Cabot Lodge, Burton K. Wheeler, Alf M. Landon, Palmer Hoyt, Herbert Lundy, Robert Notson, John D. M. Hamilton, Grace Townsend, Mark Hatfield, Homer Fergeson, James A. Farley, Rexford G. Tugwell, James H. Rowe, Thomas Corcoran, Robert S. Allen, James Roosevelt, Gardner Cowles, John S. Knight, and Harold Stassen. Their reminiscences about McNary were an indispensable contribution.

In my research, I also drew on the knowledge of Thomas Vaughan, executive director of the Oregon Historical Society. My editor, Bruce Taylor Hamilton, and his associate, Stephanie Smith, made many useful suggestions and contributed inestimably to the preparation of this biography. Another Western Imprints' staff member, Colleen Campbell, designed this jacket for this publication.

Finally, I want to thank my wife, Susan, and my two daughters, Erin and Shannon, for their patience, understanding and support during this long project.

Prologue

CHARLES Linza McNary went to the United States Senate soon
after America entered World War I, and he remained there for
more than twenty-six years. The tall, slender, sandy-haired
Oregonian would become one of the most influential legislators
of the century. His career spanned the Progressive era, the debate over the League of Nations, the Great Depression, and
World War II. He served as the Senate's Republican leader
longer than anyone before or since. His Democratic counterpart, the late Alben Barkley of Kentucky, described him as a
legislative genius. Harry Truman said that McNary was the
hardest-working and most effective member of the Senate. Both
Franklin D. Roosevelt and Herbert Hoover viewed him as a potential president of the United States. In 1940, he ran with
Wendell L. Willkie as the Republican candidate for vice president, an office he dismissed as "a damn totem pole." Being a
senator was the only job he really wanted.

Richard L. Neuberger said that McNary was to Oregon what
Thomas Jefferson must have been to Virginia—the dominant
political figure of his time. McNary was born when Ulysses S.
Grant was still president, and grew up on his family's pioneer
homestead. Orphaned at an early age, he remained sensitive all
his life to the plight of the poor, and had little patience with
public officials who did not show compassion in hard times. He
studied at Stanford in the 1890s and went on to become dean of
the Willamette University law school in his hometown. An avid

farmer, he developed the American filbert and the imperial prune, and never lost his enthusiasm for the soil.

As a young justice on the Oregon supreme court, he was the author of opinions on workmen's compensation and the eight-hour day, which were milestones in establishing basic rights for the American worker. In a statewide primary election, he was defeated for renomination to the court by a single vote. Had he won the election, McNary might well have stayed on the bench for life. Three years later, he was appointed to the Senate following the death of Harry Lane.

McNary was always a believer in the small-town values of the Pacific Northwest, and was mistrustful of Wall Street, big business, and urban political machines. "I"'ve always cast my lot with the voting groups of my state and section," he said in 1940, "and I've found if they consider me the guardian of their interests, they'll allow me considerable independence on questions that don't affect them." Partly because of where he came from, McNary became the Senate's foremost conservationist, writing laws that protected the national forests and set aside millions of acres of trees for future generations. "An orchardist," he explained, "learns to respect the laws of nature." When the Depression struck the farm belt in the early 1920s, McNary helped launch the battle for farm relief and emerged as a leading spokesman of rural America. From the beginning of his political career, he advocated public ownership of water power, and he was the father of Bonneville dam on the Columbia river.

Through years of experience and his matchless knowledge of parliamentary maneuvering, he would become the Senate's master politician. While some critics denounced him as lacking principle, Joseph Alsop favorably compared McNary to Talleyrand as a great compromiser. Although the Oregon senator was sometimes described as the last of the old western progressives, he was neither liberal nor conservative but a pragmatist who devoted his energies to getting results. "Halfway between the extremes is usually the point of wisdom," McNary declared.

On the floor of the Senate, McNary seldom rose to speak. But it was said that he could accomplish more by standing up, shooting his starched white cuffs, and saying a few words than his eloquent colleagues could do in hours of oratory. Presidents and senators of both parties sought his advice. Even though he was the leader of the Republican opposition during the New Deal, McNary made a good friend of FDR. The Democratic president had such respect for the Oregon senator that he confided to a member of his cabinet that he wanted McNary as his vice president on a bipartisan wartime unity ticket. It was McNary who blocked FDR's 1937 attempt to reorganize the Supreme Court, and who gave Roosevelt the critical support which enabled the United States to send Great Britain fifty destroyers in the summer of 1940 to help defend the island against Nazi Germany.

Throughout his Senate career, McNary held strong views on foreign policy which carried much weight and yet he never embarked beyond the shores of North America. As a freshman senator, he worked with Woodrow Wilson in an effort to salvage the Versailles Treaty and U. S. participation in the League of Nations. As an isolationist in the 1930s, he underestimated the threat of Nazi Germany and predicted there would not be a major war. Unlike most of his isolationist brethren, McNary was responsive to changing events. When Hitler's armies swallowed Western Europe, the Oregon Republican voted for the nation's first peacetime draft and Lend-Lease aid for the embattled allies. Outraged by the persecution of European Jews, McNary was co-chairman of a national organization supporting a Jewish homeland in Palestine. Seeking to prevent a divisive debate similar to the storm he had been through after World War I, McNary endorsed FDR's concept of a United Nations organization.

He was a man of simple tastes. He played tennis well into his sixties, golfed with his Senate cronies, and was a devoted baseball fan. He was a voracious reader, mostly in the field of American history and biography. With other members of the Senate's inner circle, McNary conducted much of his business in the bourbon and branchwater atmosphere of his Capitol office. When his colleagues were polled on the most popular senator, McNary invariably won in a landslide. The Oregon senator's cousin, Carlton Savage, a top official in the State Department, once asked him why his colleagues held him in such high esteem. McNary replied, "I always keep my word."

In the summer of 1882, McNary was riding his tricycle around his North Salem neighborhood. One year later, he was orphaned and would be raised by his older sisters. (Author's collection)

1

Formative Years

CHARLES Linza McNary was born 12 June 1874 on the farm that his ox-driving, maternal grandfather had homesteaded five miles north of Salem. The third son and ninth of ten children of Hugh Linza McNary and Mary Claggett McNary, he was named after Charles Claggett, who had crossed the plains in 1852 and settled on this tract. Claggett's farmhouse was surrounded by wide lawns and gardens and towering Douglas firs that had been growing before the voyage of Columbus. The boy's other grandfather, James McNary, had been captain of an 1845 wagon train that brought more than 100 families to the Pacific Northwest. Throughout his life, Charles McNary was acutely conscious of the role his family had played in the settlement of the Oregon Country.

By 1874, Salem was a prosperous agricultural center with signs of growing into a healthy metropolis. Among its newest buildings were the three-story Reed Opera House, the Ladd & Bush Bank, the fashionable Chemeketa House hotel, and the towered, French Renaissance-style Marion County Courthouse. A new state capitol would soon be constructed. Along the Willamette River, large white steamboats, puffing black smoke and white steam, shuttled passengers and freight to points north and south. The musical whistles of the Oregon and California railroad had only recently brought Salem into the locomotive age.

Hugh McNary grew up on the family homestead near the mouth of the Clackamas River. As a young man, he worked on his father's farm, operated a brickyard in Oregon City, and taught school in Linn County. In 1860 he married Mary Margaret Claggett and was given 112 acres of choice farmland from his father-in-law in the Keizer bottom section north of Salem. The McNarys raised their children as a close-knit family but Charles would have only vague memories of his mother. Frail and delicate, Mary died before her youngest son's fourth birthday. Following the death of his wife, Hugh moved the family into Salem and bought a variety store. By this time his own health was declining and he could no longer manage the farm tract. Though the retail business proved to be less strenuous than the farm, Hugh never managed to regain his once robust health. On 18 July 1883, he died at the age of fifty-three. Charles was nine years old.

As the youngest son, Charles was known as "Tot" and family members would always address him by that nickname. He was a handsome child with blue eyes and almost lemon-hued hair. To a small boy, Salem provided an exciting and stimulating environment and Charles acquired a wide range of interests. On the farm, he picked fruit and vegetables and put them into baskets to be sold at his grandfather's grocery store. From an early age, he demonstrated a wry sense of humor. When a neighbor saw him chasing around a corn crib, he asked what the boy was doing. "Catching mice," McNary replied. Asked how many he had, Charles said, "When I get this blamed dodger and two more, I will have three."

When McNary was six, he started attending classes at the little one-room Keizer schoolhouse. Carrying his lunch in a tin pail, he cut across his grandfather's meadows, through some brush, and along a dusty path. One of his first teachers was a man named Royal with a reputation as a strict disciplinarian. McNary was paddled more than once. "Everybody gets lickings at school," he said years later. "It's customary with all boys who live to be men." Charles transferred to Salem's Central School when the family moved into town. By then he was developing a thirst for knowledge and for reading that he would never lose.

The McNarys lived on North Commercial Street and the whole neighborhood was a playground. A short distance away was North Mill Creek, a popular swimming hole. Boon's Island, an abandoned lot next to the creek and the old Jason Lee home, was the baseball diamond. Charles showed early promise as an athlete, playing with other energetic youngsters from the neighborhood.

Following his father's death, Charles was raised by his older sisters and brother. At the age of twenty-six, Nina McNary became the family matriarch. The family members, she later recalled, were "kept together as best they would." In an era when higher education for women was still rare, Nina had studied and graduated from Willamette University. Though she had taught school, Nina put aside her career and devoted her full energies to her younger siblings. Other family members took jobs to help pay household expenses. Martha, the next eldest sister, taught in Salem public schools. And the older brother, John Hugh McNary, joined the *Oregon Statesman* as a reporter.

Through his brother's recommendation, Charles was hired as a *Statesman* paper boy. "I delivered the *Statesman* in North Salem," he would later recall. "My paper route extended from Marion Square northward to the Scotch mills owned by William S. Ladd." He contributed to the family's income in other ways. "I would drive the neighbors' cows out to pasture in North Salem after I had delivered my papers and in the late afternoon would go out and drive them back again, seeing that each of them got home in good time to be milked. I got a dollar a month per head, and I usually handled about ten cows."

In the summertime, he rode five miles each day to work in the fruit orchards of Adolph Wertz, the German-American who was one of the Willamette Valley's pioneer orchardists. McNary's duties included budding, grafting and tying the apples. Charles enjoyed working with trees so much that it would become a life-long passion. As a high school student he earned $1.15 a day by working in a downtown tree nursery across the street from the capitol. While watching state legislators coming and going, Charles gradually began to show an interest in politics.

During this period, McNary became acquainted with another orphan boy his own age with whom he shared a political destiny. His name was Herbert Clark Hoover. A native of Iowa, Hoover had moved to Newberg, Oregon, following the death of his parents. Hoover was raised by an uncle, Henry Minthorn. In 1888, Minthorn moved to Salem and established the Oregon Land Company, where Hoover worked as a office boy. "He was a funny-looking little fellow with a short neck and a round head which was always surmounted by a funny little round hat," recalled an office secretary who called Hoover "the quietest, most efficient, and most industrious boy I ever knew."

Hoover struck McNary as quiet, reserved, and not much fun. "Bert Hoover used to come in from Highland addition," McNary recalled years later, "so we saw each other frequently. He was much too interested in geology and in his studies to have time to do much playing, so he never joined us when we went swimming in the Willamette or when we played ball."

McNary loved the outdoors. Strong, healthy, and physically daring, he became a star athlete. Baseball was his favorite game, and McNary rose from the neighborhood sandlot to pitch and play first base for Salem's city team. "As twirler for the Salem nine, McNary won almost every game in which his team crossed bats with a state club," David Hazen later wrote in the *Oregonian*. "He was a natural-born baseball player—fast, graceful, fearless. And McNary was a great hitter." Some contemporaries suggested that McNary might have had a professional baseball career if he had not gone into law practice. He retained his enthusiasm for the game and, in later years, made friendships with major league stars Walter Johnson and Ty Cobb.

John McNary planned to practice law and encouraged his younger brother to join him. The elder brother studied at the University of Oregon and returned to Salem, becoming city editor of the *Statesman*. In 1890 John was elected Marion County recorder on the Republican ticket and confided to a newspaper colleague that the position would give him more time to prepare for a legal career. The new county recorder hired his brother as a clerk. "On several occasions he fired me," Charles said many years later, "but he would always take me back because of a deep affection."

Charles enrolled briefly at Capital Business College but found the courses dull and monotonous. His academic performance was uninspired and he soon withdrew. Later, he took prepatory courses at Willamette University and studied more diligently. His ambition was to attend either the University of California or the newly established Stanford University. So he turned down his grandfather's offer to take over the thriving family grocery business.

In January 1896 McNary organized a social dance club whose thirty-seven charter members included three future Oregon governors—Oswald West, Ben Olcott, and Isaac Patterson. McNary was elected secretary-treasurer of the club and kept membership records and minutes of the meetings in a green ledger. Their social functions were well attended and featured such period tunes as "After the Ball," "The Band Played On," and "Sweet Rosie O'Grady." McNary's most frequent date was the attractive Jessie Breyman, daughter of Salem's leading merchant.

McNary and Oswald West once debated before a local debating society. Prior to the debate, McNary received some coaching from Frank Davey, a newspaper reporter. "I don't remember whether Os won or I did," McNary said years later. "I was nearly scared to death and my knees seemed as if they had turned to water. They would hardly hold me up. My only consolation was that Os was also badly scared. I was so rattled I didn't pretend to pay any attention to what he was saying and I very much doubt whether Os tried to answer any of my arguments."

McNary decided to enroll at Stanford University in the fall of 1896, influenced by the example of Herbert Hoover, who had already worked his way through Stanford. "I figured that if he could find something to do, I could, too," McNary later told an interviewer. McNary sailed from Portland to San Francisco on the elegant steamship *Columbia*. As a result of the rate war between steamship companies and the railroads, his first-class ticket, including meals, was just five dollars.

Entering Stanford as a full-time student, McNary settled into Encina Hall and supported himself by waiting on tables in a dining room. McNary boasted that he could carry five plates of roast beef faster than anyone. With practice he learned to balance three plates on one arm and three tumblers on the other. As a working student he was a "barb," ineligible for the social activities sponsored by the "frats," Stanford's elite fraternity crowd. McNary resented the caste system, friends said, but he seldom complained about it. "There are lots of fellows who were going to dances that you never hear of now," he observed many years later.

Railroad mogul Leland Stanford had founded the university as a memorial to his son, with the hope that it would become the Harvard of the west. The school's progressive academic atmosphere and Leland Stanford's money would soon make it one of the nation's foremost institutions of higher education. McNary studied law, history, science, and economics there.

For McNary, the high point of his first semester was a campus lecture by his political hero, U.S. House Speaker Thomas

Brackett Reed. The Maine Republican was renowned for his caustic wit and McNary kept a scrapbook of Reed's epigrams. "A statesman," Reed said, "is a politician who is dead." Several months prior to his Stanford visit, Reed had been edged out for the GOP presidential nomination by William McKinley, whom he said had "no more backbone than a chocolate eclair."

"I think the greatest thrill of Charley's life came that fall when he listened to Tom Reed," said Stanford classmate Phil Metschan. "When it was announced that Reed was going to speak on campus, McNary got all his lessons away in advance and did his table work ahead of time. Then he got a place as near the Speaker as he could get, and he was the most interested listener Reed had."

The house speaker impressed upon McNary the importance of brevity in public speaking. "He is a dull fellow who cannot tell all he knows on a subject in thirty minutes," said Reed. More than forty years later, McNary was still quoting Reed's advice to the Stanford undergraduates.

Few students appreciated history as much as McNary. His reading of history and biography included Gibbon and Plutarch. McNary was stirred to his most energetic efforts in Professor Shaw's course in Roman history. In the winter of 1897, the 23-year-old McNary wrote an essay about agrarian reformer Spurius Cassius that revealed his own political views:

"Cassius was a consul but was a rare and good patriot. He tried to deal with this land question with fairness and to distribute it among all classes of people. He is the first one of those magnanimous patriots who rose above his party and sowed the virtuous seeds of equal welfare. He was a statesman. . . . His laws were eradicated, but their principle enjoyed perpetuity. His principle was enormous."

McNary was studying so intensively that he did not try out for the university's baseball team. That spring his family urged him to return to Salem and complete his education at Willamette. His brother John offered him a clerkship in his law office with the promise of a full partnership. Charles, after much deliberation, accepted the offer and returned to Oregon.

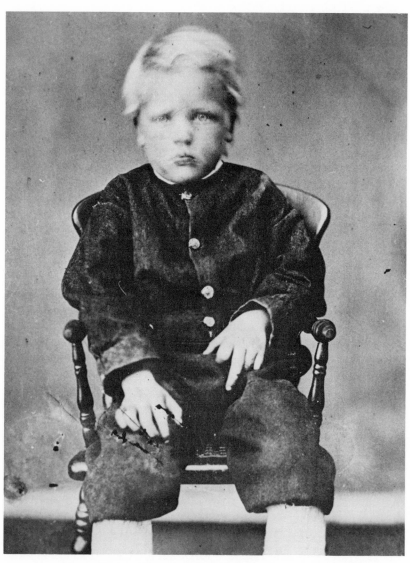

At the age of four, Charles Linza McNary posed for this tintype portrait in a Salem studio, 1878. (Author's collection)

The McNary home (top) on North Commercial Street in Salem, ca. 1890. From left to right, Nina, Martha, and Ella, and, in a swing, Charles. Standing in the left background are Earnest Porter, who lived with the McNarys, and John.

McNary and his 1895 high school graduating class (bottom). McNary is third from left, back row. Seventy years later, the city's third high school would be named in McNary's honor. (Both author's collection)

8

2

Salem Lawyer

FOR MORE THAN a year, Charles read law in his brother's office. Passing the bar examination without difficulty, he was admitted to the Oregon Bar in 1898. As promised, John made his younger brother a full partner in the firm of McNary & McNary.

Seven years older than Charles, John H. McNary had been practicing law since 1894. During his term as county recorder, John spent evenings studying law in the library of George H. Burnett, a prominent Salem lawyer and future chief justice of the Oregon Supreme Court. On leaving the county courthouse, John went into law practice with Sam L. Hayden. With John managing the campaign, Hayden was elected Marion County district attorney in 1898. John became Hayden's deputy district attorney and, though still associated with the law firm, delegated much of the responsibility to Charles.

The McNary law firm grew rapidly, helped in no small part by John's official position. Handling property transactions became the younger McNary's legal specialty and he built a sizable clientele. He was soon teaching a course in property law at Willamette University. In the spring, Charles played first base for the town baseball team, but with his expanding law practice there was less time for social activities.

Even so, he was much in demand as one of Salem's most eligible young bachelors. Tall and slender with well-chiseled features, McNary took pride in his appearance and dressed in sartorial style. Although he dated other women, McNary was becoming more and more interested in the cultivated and charming Jessie Breyman. Her father, Belgian immigrant Eugene Breyman, had built a small pioneer store into Salem's most thriving business. McNary acknowledged that the Breymans "took high rank in the business and social world" and he enjoyed their company.

While courting Jessie, Charles often visited at her family's imposing Victorian mansion at the corner of Church and Court streets. In the Breyman parlor, McNary played the piano and sang tunes of the period. "I used to sing an old song in dulcet tones," McNary recalled, "'Absence makes the heart grow fonder; that is why I long for you.' That old song, and 'Say, Au Revoir,' and 'Cast Aside,' gave voice to the expression, Charlie McNary, the sweet canary."

On 19 November 1902, Charles and Jessie were married beneath a floral arch in the front parlor of the Breyman mansion. A local newspaper described it as "one of the prettiest home weddings that has taken place in the capital city this season." Following the ceremony, the young couple greeted 70 guests in the large formal dining room. "The bride and groom are well known and very popular in Salem," the *Statesman* reported. "The bride is a highly educated and accomplished young lady, and a leader in social circles in this city, while the groom is a talented young attorney with a bright future before him."

For their honeymoon, Charles and Jessie escaped to the banks of the Columbia and stayed in several lodges for ten days. On their return, they lived for a short time at the Breyman home. As a wedding gift, Jessie's parents had a home built for them on an adjacent lot. And, a few months later, Charles and Jessie moved into their new house on Court Street.

It was a storybook marriage. Like her husband, Jessie had a teasing humor and a warmth that made her an engaging companion. "Jessie was delightful," said McNary's niece, Margaret Marshall. "She was absolutely devoted to my uncle as he was to her." Jessie encouraged McNary's political ambitions and gave him reassurance when he was troubled. They frequently entertained other young couples and their own large families. On weekends, they had picnics at the old Claggett farm, which McNary had bought back into the family with help from his brother-in-law Walter Stolz. McNary took Jessie on far-flung vacations, including a 1904 trip to Cuba and the southeastern United States.

In 1904 Charles managed his brother's successful campaign for district attorney and was appointed his chief deputy. Thirty years old and an extremely hard worker, Charles was a vigorous prosecutor who won considerable renown in the courtroom. An editorial in a Salem newspaper said that the younger McNary "is entitled to much credit for the manner in which he conducts the prosecution thereof, and not only earns the respect that is due him for his rare legal ability, but carries his points and wins his cases against such overwhelming odds."

Meanwhile, McNary was taking on additional teaching responsibilities at Willamette's law school. In 1908, on the retirement of John W. Reynolds, McNary was appointed dean of the school. Until McNary's appointment, the law school had no home and classes were taught in downtown law offices. He soon transformed the school from a loosely attached appendage of the university into one of its most prestigious departments. Dean McNary moved the law school to the campus and implemented a broader curriculum. A brochure said, "the members of the Bar of the Capital of Oregon take great pride in the Law Department of the Willamette University and it is no doubt one of the best Law Departments on the Pacific Coast, and students wishing to equip themselves thoroughly for the legal profession will do well to consider this department of the University before going elsewhere." McNary was an effective recruiter. In 1908, only four students had graduated with law degrees at spring commencement. Within five years, there was a graduating class of thirty-six law students.

During McNary's tenure as dean, Most of his faculty members were prominent lawyers, including I. H. Van Winkle, who would later become Oregon's attorney general. Though the law school depended upon tuition fees for all financial support, McNary made it his policy that no student would be denied an education for lack of funds. On numerous occasions he gave students personal checks to cover their tuition and board. Some of the more solemn faculty members at the conservative Methodist university frowned on McNary's participation in beer parties with his students, yet his critics acknowledged that he was the man most responsible for Willamette's new-found eminence among law schools.

"Mr. McNary has one ruling passion," reported a Portland newspaper, "which he talks of more than anything else. This hobby is to make Willamette Law College one of the largest, most thorough and most widely recognized institutions of its kind in the United States."

At the same time, he was winning personal recognition as a horticulturist and farmer. On his family farm, McNary raised trees of all varieties and experimented with such techniques as cross-breeding, hybridization, and grafting. With Jessie, he traveled to California and inspected the nurseries of botanists Luther Burbank and Felix Gillette. He bought 50 young filbert trees from Gillette that had been imported from Barcelona. By 1909, McNary had transformed the Spanish seedlings into the first commercial filbert orchard in the nation. He also developed the Imperial prune, the largest and sweetest variety of the fruit as well as some of the Willamette Valley's prize cherries and walnuts. "In those days," said McNary, "I used to drive the five miles to the farm every afternoon, to work until dark in the orchards. I shaped a thousand trees with my own hands."

McNary described the development of the American filbert in a series of articles published in the *Statesman*.

Experiments with haphazard plantings have demonstrated that western Oregon contains a perfectly wholesome climate for the culture of filberts, comparable in every way to the regions surrounding the Mediterranean sea where they are grown to perfection.

All attempts at cultivation of filberts in this country have failed save in the western parts of Oregon, Washington, and the northern part of California. Here in Oregon, we have the open winter which is a guarantee of immunity to winter killing of the trees and here can be found the same moist river-bottom lands and rolling hills that obtain in the genial climate by the Mediterranean.

Widely reprinted in pamphlet form, McNary's articles introduced filberts to many farmers in Oregon and Washington. The *Statesman* reported that McNary refused payment for his series, declaring that his hope was to make the filbert one of Oregon's major crops. The Pacific Northwest soon became the leading producer of the American filbert.

In an effort to promote local agricultural interests, McNary organized the Salem Fruit Union in 1909 and would remain its president for the rest of his life. He felt that the organization of such groups to exchange information, discuss prices, and promote their products would benefit consumer and producer.

McNary was elected president of the Salem Board of Trade in 1909. He moved the board of Trade offices from a small room at City Hall to larger quarters on State Street with display windows for home-produced commodities. As president, McNary lobbied for reduced freight rates for Salem area agricultural products.

An early supporter of public power, McNary led a revolt in the Salem commercial club against the choking off of waterfalls by private power corporations. He backed the "Oregon System" reforms of William U'Ren—the initiative, recall, referendum, primary elections, and the direct election of U. S. senators. U'Ren, a blacksmith, made Oregon a national showcase for reform during the Progressive Era. The slight, soft-spoken U'Ren was nationally renowned as "The Lawgiver". His efforts were responsible for progressive laws in a half dozen other states. Lincoln Steffens proclaimed him as the nation's most influential reformer.

Politically, McNary was a Republican progressive and he chose to work within his party. In 1910, many GOP progressives bolted the party in favor of Democratic gubernatorial candidate Oswald West, McNary's boyhood friend. But McNary resisted the trend. When West won the governorship, he named McNary as special counsel for the state railroad commission. In that post, McNary pressed for lower passenger and freight rates.

In 1912, McNary supported President William Howard Taft's re-election against Theodore Roosevelt's insurgent challenge, serving as president of the local Taft-Sherman club. Democrat Woodrow Wilson captured the presidency because of the Taft-Roosevelt split. In Oregon, McNary maintained friendly relations with both factions of the Republican party, while remaining on the best of terms with Governor West. He had been urged to run for Congress earlier in the year, but McNary was not yet ready to take the political plunge.

13

For a local civic pageant, McNary (top left) donned a costume from America's revolutionary period. Playing the piano in the Breyman mansion (top right), McNary specialized in turn-of-the-century favorites. Even before their marriage, Jessie Breyman (bottom left) and McNary (bottom right) were among Salem's most popular young couples. (All author's collection)

John McNary, ca. 1900. (Author's collection)

Jessie Breyman McNary, ca. 1910. (Author's collection)

3

Mr. Justice McNary

IN THE SPRING of 1913, the Oregon Legislature debated a
bill that would expand the supreme court from five to seven justices. On a morning walk to the capitol, Governor West encountered John McNary and made a proposition which he recounted
years later in the *Oregon Historical Quarterly*. "John, you better
get up to the State House and help the Multnomah crowd increase the Supreme Court membership," the governor began.
"If they put it over, I will appoint you as one of the new judges."

"Oh don't do that," replied John. "Appoint Charley."

When the legislation passed, West did just that, announcing
the appointments of Charles L. McNary and McMinnville lawyer William M. Ramsey. At thirty-eight, McNary was the youngest member of the high court and a Salem newspaper called
him the "Baby Justice." Yet his legal stature was unquestioned.
"The appointment of Mr. McNary," declared the *Oregonian*, "is
hailed with approval of the entire bar of the state, and of the
young attorney's hundreds of lay friends."

McNary took the appointment at a financial sacrifice. His law
firm, reported a Portland newspaper, was "considered the biggest in the state south of Portland." A Salem newspaper added
that McNary could have earned much more money had he remained in private practice. "He felt that the experience on the
bench would be of great benefit," the report stated, "and that
the honor, coming to him so early in life, was one he could not
turn down."

For McNary, the bench offered challenge and responsibility. He soon established himself as a judicial activist and strong advocate of progressive reform. "I have endeavored to interpret the law as a progressive science rather than as a rule too old to be corrected if found inapplicable to present-day decisions," McNary wrote during his first year on the Supreme Court.

Oregon had been a national catalyst for social reform. An Oregon law passed in 1903 had limited women to work days of ten hours. As with many progressive reforms, it seemed in danger of judicial nullification when the case of *Muller* v. *Oregon* reached the conservative U.S. Supreme Court. But it was Oregon's good fortune to be represented by Louis D. Brandeis, the legendary "people's advocate." In his brief, Brandeis put little emphasis on legal tradition and concentrated on sociological, economic, and medical evidence that long hours of work were damaging to the health and safety of women. When the court sustained the Oregon law, it was a judicial landmark that declared the power of courts to take cognizance of the circumstances of industrial abuses. Over the next decade, 39 states adopted new laws based on the Oregon decision.

Within the Progressive movement, there were sharp disagreements over the role of labor unions. Herbert Croly, founding editor of the *New Republic*, denounced organized labor as "arrogant and lawless." McNary credited trade unions with making dramatic gains for the working class through social legislation. In a 1912 Labor Day speech, McNary called on union members to mobilize and concentrate their efforts on improving working conditions. McNary described Oregon's 1911 Employer's Liability Law as the crowning achievement in the progress of justice to labor.

The speech sealed a relationship. Organized labor would support McNary throughout his public career. The *Portland Labor Press* hailed "the discovery of such an able and outspoken champion."

In his first month on the court, McNary wrote the majority opinion in an occupational-safety case, *Graves* v. *Portland Railway, Light and Power Company*. While laying street-paving blocks at a Portland intersection, a worker had been struck and seriously injured by a streetcar. Disclaiming responsibility, the railway company said the worker had been careless. McNary rejected the antiquated common-law doctrines that had stipulated the company was not responsible if a worker had assumed the risks of his job. "It must occur to a reasonable mind," wrote Judge McNary, "that in this age of strenuous endeavor, in order to do efficient work and to scant not the measure thereof, the individual toiler must pursue his employment sometimes to the utter engrossment of his faculties, and, realizing the present necessity of concentration, the courts of modern thought have announced the rule that persons engaged in work upon the public streets are not called upon to exercise the same diligence in avoiding accidents as pedestrians who use the street merely as a medium of locomotion."

McNary consistently defended the rights of injured workers in similar cases and was not hesitant about using the bench as an instrument for social change. He wrote the opinion upholding the Employer's Liability Law, holding that industry had an obligation to compensate injured or incapacitated workers. In *Askatin* v. *McInnis & Reed Co.*, McNary held the company responsible for defective equipment.

Strongly backed by Governor West, the 1913 Oregon legislature established an Industrial Welfare Commission to regulate wages, hours, and the safety, health and welfare of workers. The commission promptly established a minimum-wage requirement for factory and store employees. Corporate interests challenged the panel's legitimacy and Brandeis filed a brief defending the statute. With McNary arguing forcefully on its behalf, the commission's legality was sustained by a unanimous decision of the Oregon court. The statute was later upheld by the United States Supreme Court.

Justice McNary wrote the opinion which upheld the 1913 law regulating eight-hour work days for public employees. In defiance of the new law, R. E. Lee Steiner, superintendent of the Oregon State Hospital, forced workers to put in longer hours. When Steiner was arrested, he claimed the law violated the "due process" clause of the Fourteenth Amendment. It was the same argument that corporate interests had used to persuade courts to thwart innovative social legislation. Charles McNary, however, held that the state had acted within its police powers. It was perfectly proper, McNary wrote, for the state of Oregon to "inaugurate a rule of conduct not to work its employees more than eight hours a day, and legally direct its instrumentalities of government faithfully to observe such a mandate. The terms of the employment are by this statute publicly proclaimed."

In *Spende* v. *Western Life Co.*, McNary ruled that an insurance company had attempted to cheat an elderly man out of his annuity. "In contracts of this nature," said McNary, "there is almost a sacred duty of performance as they frequently act as a bridge that spans the chasm between penury and well-being."

McNary also wrote the opinion upholding a law that prohibited county treasurers from depositing public funds in favorite banks and sharing kickbacks on the interest. "A remedy is needed for existing abuse," wrote McNary. "The essence of the statute is to establish county depositories and to divert into the public exchequer, moneys in the way of interest that has heretofore flowed into private reservoirs."

More than anything, Justice McNary's opinions demonstrated his compassion for people and their individual rights. "He seemed to get down to the human right of the matter and let the fine points of the law go to smash," wrote a capital correspondent.

McNary outlined his judicial philosophy in his dissenting cide the law correctly so far as it lies within the human mind. The next duty is to smite that rule of human action which is found to be unjust, however well it may be buttressed by precedent. Great reluctance to overthrow an established doctrine would naturally proceed from an established rule where property rights or individual liberty were at stake; but, where neither one nor the other of these long-respected rights have been entrenched by reason of judicial utterance, no hesitation should deter one from uprooting that rule which he believes to be subversive of common justice." It was the clearest and most complete definition of McNary's approach to law as he had intended it to be.

During the winter of 1914, the Oregon Supreme Court moved into a stately white marble building with tiled floors, and hand-carved paneling. On 2 March 1914, the court held its first session in its new chambers. For the first time in Oregon's history, the justices wore flowing black robes. It was an atmosphere that McNary found eminently satisfying.

So it was not surprising that McNary filed for the Republican nomination for a full term in the 15 May primary. Eight candidates filed for four positions, including Chief Justice Thomas

McBride and Justice Henry J. Bean. It had been a court tradition that sitting justices did not actively campaign.

"In the campaign I am somewhat handicapped by the fact I cannot leave my work and make a political campaign without exposing myself to deserved criticism," McNary wrote S. R. Cash on 30 April 1914. "I must, therefore, in a large way, leave my case with sincere friends, and those people in the state who believe I have made good."

He received strong labor support. The Central Labor Council of Salem endorsed him as a champion of labor. So, too, did other union organizations. When McNary was urged by his campaign chairman to wage a more partisan campaign, he refused. "If you can't play the game fairly," he said, "let's don't play."

McNary, however, was actively working behind the scenes to further his candidacy. He sent campaign literature, letters, and photographs to every daily and weekly newspaper in Oregon. In personal letters to farmers, he wrote, "I have long been identified with the fruit and farming interests of the state. . . . As you are aware of the immense value of these resources, I think it is imperative that the highest court in the state should have representation familiar with and possessing knowledge of the farming interests which are frequently the subject of important litigation."

On May 2, McNary made one of his rare campaign appearances at a Portland banquet that had been organized by his former law students. In his remarks, McNary suggested that his former Willamette students begin holding annual meetings.

It was soon apparent on election night that justices McBride, Bean, and Lawrence T. Harris had won three of the four Republican nominations. McNary and Judge Henry L. Benson of Klamath Falls were in a virtual dead heat for the remaining nomination. Benson had narrowly carried Multnomah County, but McNary ran strongly in the Willamette Valley.

On 18 May, the *Oregonian* reported McNary had moved into a 600-vote lead. Late returns from rural precincts, though, eroded McNary's margin. And, a day later, it was reported that Benson was in front by 20 votes. The lead changed several times over the next week with McNary the chief beneficiary. Finally, Secretary of State Ben Olcott announced on 5 June that McNary had won by 13 votes. McNary's nomination was to be certified by Governor West on 13 June.

However, Judge Benson, demanded a recount and McNary agreed. "I do not feel that either of us can accept this nomination with a shadow of doubt upon the vote," said McNary.

On 22 June, the revised count showed McNary and Benson in a tie. The *Oregonian* suggested, "McNary and Benson might split the salary and divide the work." The deadlock continued until 24 August when Benson gained a single vote in Grant County. Then, on 26 August, it was discovered that 15 ballots in the Sixes precinct of Curry County had been uncounted.

Governor West asked both candidates for an extension of the recount until the Sixes votes could be included. The State Canvassing board was scheduled to certify the winner on 5 September. Judge Benson, unwilling to risk his one-vote lead, vetoed West's proposal.

At the board meeting, West disclosed that McNary had asked for recounts in a half a dozen precincts and Benson had done the same in 19 precincts. Although McNary had all of his counted, Benson quit after only two of his designated precincts had been rechecked. A. C. Emmons, representing Benson, said, "McNary had a right to count his and we had a right to count or not count ours."

McNary felt that his opponent had been less than honorable.

We entered into a stipulation for the recount of precincts [McNary told the board], and one was ahead one day, and the next the other, and finally we were tied. Then a second stipulation was entered into and I was told by Mr. Emmons that Judge Benson would have five or six precincts, and I inserted six. After I had signed and forwarded the stipulation, Mr. Emmons called me over the telephone and said he would have 19 or 20 and said he might want to withdraw a few. I conceded to the insertion of a clause permitting the withdrawal of a few of the precincts, but it was never my understanding that he was to withdraw all or most of them. I proceeded with a recount of my precincts in good faith. Judge Benson did not even procure a court order for a recount of the two precincts he recounted, but I did. No move was made by Mr. Emmons or Judge Benson to recount their precincts. That is anything but fair.

But I do not want to quibble over this office [McNary concluded]. I am willing to abide by the decision of the Board. I would not accept the nomination with a single vote uncounted, but I enter no protest.

Once again, the board asked Benson for a two-week extension so that the Sixes votes could be included in the official count. For the second time, Benson declined. Unable to count the Sixes ballots without Benson's consent, the board declared him the GOP nominee by a single vote. When friends urged him to force a recount through a court order, McNary replied, "To hell with it."

Governor West signed Benson's certificate of nomination under protest. In a blistering letter, West accused Benson of trickery in his handling of the recount:

> While I am firm in my conviction that a complete and correct return of the votes cast at the election, or even of those precincts where errors have been reported, would have shown Judge McNary and not yourself to be the successful candidate, you have succeeded, through sharp practices and methods which would put to blush the meanest pettifogger in the land, in producing a result upon the face of the returns which leaves this office no alternative, but that of issuing you the certificate.
>
> As a circuit judge [West continued], you have many times sent to jail young men who have happened to trespass, in a small way, upon the property rights of others. Yet today, you trample upon the birthright of a whole people, and because you have been skillful enough to keep within the law, you are permitted not only to go your own way unmolested, but to sit in judgment upon your fellow man. It is this lack of equality before the law which creates discontent and leads many to believe that the law is like a cobweb where small flies are caught and the great ones break through.
>
> The cloud under which you secured your nomination will follow you always [the governor asserted]. Day by day as you sit upon the bench and are reminded that a man must come into court with clean hands, you will be haunted by the ghost of the past and as your thoughts revert to uncounted precincts, the clock upon the wall will seem to tick out 'Sixes, Sixes, Sixes' and you will bow your head in shame.

Graceful in defeat, McNary endorsed Judge Benson. During the long weeks of uncertainty about his future, McNary performed actively on the court. In one of his last opinions, *Kalich* v. *Knapp*, McNary further outlined his philosophy of government. "The source—the abiding place of sovereignty—is in the people. Government is merely an agency by which it is exercised. The legislative body is but a component of that agency— a contrivance by which the people crystallize their ideas into the form of legislation."

Leaving the court in January 1915, McNary and his wife took a long vacation in Central America, the West Indies, and Virginia Beach, Virginia. It was their first real vacation in years and McNary took letters of introduction from Oregon's new governor, James Withycombe, Chief Justice McBride, and the Catholic archbishop of Oregon.

McNary acknowledged that defeat had been painful. "The world had fallen in on me," he told Richard L. Neuberger years later. "I was tormented by the knowledge that I would have won if only I had shaken several more hands, if I had gone to the pioneers' picnic which I had missed because of a headache, if I had taken time to write a couple of additional letters to acquaintances. I was about to withdraw from public life completely, when I began to think that these reasons made it all the more imperative that I keep on trying. If such trivial things could explain my defeat, the next time I would surely win."

John McNary preceded his younger brother into politics and was the Oregon senator's alter ego and chief political advisor. (Author's collection)

For Justice of the
Supreme Court

CHARLES L. McNARY

REPUBLICAN CANDIDATE

VOTE THUS:
34 X CHARLES L. McNARY

Your Vote and Support Will
Aid Me

Republican Primaries, May 15, 1914

McNary at forty, Salem, Oregon. The associate justice of the Oregon Supreme Court used this portrait in his 1914 campaign for retention. He was defeated by one vote.

(Inset) In McNary's first political race, he learned that a single vote could indeed make the difference. (Both author's collection)

McNary with Salem relatives (top), ca. 1914. Back row: McNary, Rueben Boise, Frank Snedecor, Rudloph Prael, Walter Stolz and William Brown. Front row: Mrs. McNary, Mrs. Boise, Mrs. Snedecor, Mrs. Eugene Breyman, Werner Breyman, Mrs. Prael, Mrs. Stolz and Mrs. Brown. (OHS collections)

The McNary's vacationing in Havana, 1915 (bottom). McNary took the trip after his Oregon Supreme Court term had expired. (Author's collection)

McNary's portrait for his first U.S. Senate race was taken in the Washington, D.C. studio of the prestigious firm Harris and Ewing, 1918. (Author's collection)

4
To the Senate

CHARLES McNary was determined to return to a public career. He knew that his law practice would be only partially fulfilling. His intellectual and political growth were such that he soon became bored with the conventionality of private practice. So he tried new things. He planted more than 40 acres of walnut trees on his farm and wrote about it in the *American Nut Journal*. He began organizing a cooperative selling agency in Western Oregon in an effort to eliminate the middle men and give farmers more profit for their produce. He invested in local real estate. He became secretary and counsel for Gideon Stolz Company, Salem's leading beverage distributor, which was operated by McNary's brother-in-law W. T. Stolz.

McNary's social and family life were pleasant. Jessie was always there to help him and they had more time together. Their house on Court Street was a popular gathering place for Salem's most prominent figures.

In the winter of 1916, there were published reports that McNary would challenge Congressman Willis C. Hawley in the Republican primary. McNary, however, thought it would be politically unwise to attempt a comeback so soon after his defeat. "One can go stale in politics as well as in athletics," he observed. "The man who is a candidate every year, first for this and then for that, wears himself out and wearies the public."

McNary actively supported U. S. Supreme Court Justice Charles Evans Hughes in the Oregon GOP presidential primary. Justice Hughes had refused to permit his name to be entered in other primaries, but under Oregon's unique election law could not prevent his name from going before the voters. Oregon was the final primary before the Republican convention and Hughes won impressively. Influenced by the Oregon vote, the Chicago convention drafted Hughes on the third ballot. "It was fortunate for Charles Evans Hughes that the people of Oregon could express their preference without political or legal hindrance," said McNary, "and it was equally fortunate that the agents of the people at the Chicago convention hearkened to the voice of our commonwealth and nominated him as the candidate of a united and triumphant party."

On 8 July 1916, McNary was elected Republican state chairman and took charge of the Hughes campaign in Oregon. McNary was chosen on the third ballot of a close race among a half dozen contenders, including State Representative Robert Stanfield of Umatilla County and Portland Hotel owner Phil Metschan, McNary's Stanford classmate. For two ballots, the Republican State Committee was deadlocked, with McNary leading but short of a majority. His stock rose when A. E. Clark of Portland, who had been a delegate to the Progressive national convention, said McNary would be acceptable to progressives. Walter L. Tooze, who had nominated McNary, called him a "compromise man, young, clean, active." On the third ballot, McNary received the requisite 18 votes. His selection was acclaimed by the state's editorial pages.

McNary was surprised when notified of his election by telephone. "Certainly, I shall accept," he said, "but I had no intimation of my selection as chairman until after the act was accomplished. I shall do all that I can to assist in the election of the splendid state and national ticket chosen by the electorate in the open primaries held last May. I appreciate most keenly the value of a united Republican party and therefore contemplate with pleasure the unification of the Republican and Progressive parties."

To a remarkable degree, McNary managed to bring harmony to the Oregon Hughes campaign, involving GOP regulars and progressives in the effort. In August, McNary introduced Hughes during a rally at the Ice Palace in Portland. In November, McNary's organization delivered Oregon for Hughes when President Wilson swept every other state in the Far West. Frank Davey, Marion County's GOP chairman, attributed the Hughes victory in Oregon to the selection of "a clean, advance thought, unfactional young man" as state chairman.

On election night, President Wilson had gone to bed thinking he had been defeated. Hughes had carried the large industrial states of the Northeast and Midwest and the Democatic *New York World* had announced the Republican's election. By the next morning, Wilson's huge vote in the West had erased the Hughes lead and it became apparent that California would decide who lived in the White House. According to legend, a newspaper reporter bearing the bad news to the Republican candidate's hotel suite was informed that "the President" could not be disturbed. "When he wakes up," the newsman is said to have shot back, "tell him he's no longer President."

Following his re-election on the slogan "He Kept Us Out of War," Wilson served notice that he intended to assert his leadership in world affairs. Attempting to secure a "peace without victory" in Europe's Great War, the President spent months trying to interest Germany in a League of Nations, with emphasis on freedom of the seas and universal acceptance of self-government. Germany rebuffed him. And, as for the Allies, Wilson did not believe that Britain and France were genuinely committed to democratic principles. Finally, Wilson determined that he himself would be the arbiter and peacemaker. Winston Churchill wrote, "The actions of the United States with its repercussions on the history of the world depended, during the awful period of Armageddon, upon the working of this man's mind and spirit to the exclusion of almost every other factor."

Only through intervention, Wilson concluded, would it be possible to translate his ideals into reality. Intensified German U-boat campaigns in the spring of 1917 brought him to his 2 April proclamation that the "world must be made safe for democracy." It was a war message. And Congress responded with a declaration of war against Germany.

Oregon's Democratic Senator Harry Lane was among six members of the Senate who voted against American entry into the war. The United States, they argued, was not forced into war by treaty obligations nor was it directly threatened. Lane, a former Portland mayor and grandson of Oregon's first territorial governor, was unwavering in his opposition to the war. Wilson attacked him and the other dissenters as a "little group of willful men."

It was a time of mindless jingoism. A federal judge in Texas said that the six senators should be lined up and shot for defying the president. In Oregon, recall petitions were circulated against Senator Lane by wealthy and well-organized forces that denounced him for treason. Thousands of signatures were collected.

Deeply hurt by the venom of his critics, Lane suffered a nervous breakdown and died two months after his dissenting vote. "When Harry Lane was denounced by men in public life whom he loved, as an enemy to his country, it well-nigh broke his heart," recalled Senator George Norris of Nebraska.

Almost immediately, Oregon newspapers began speculating about possible successors to Lane. Governor Withycombe assured a luncheon meeting of the Women's Suffrage Alliance that he would appoint a senator who favored national women's suffrage and prohibition. Sources in the governor's offices mentioned Judge McNary as a likely choice. Another leading possibility was said to have been *Oregonian* editor Edgar B. Piper.

It was reported in the *Portland Spectator* that the governor sounded out Piper on his availability for Lane's Senate seat. And the *Oregonian* editor later confirmed that he had indeed been approached about whether he would accept the appointment. After thinking it over, Piper decided he did not want to give up his editorship and recommended that the governor appoint Circuit Judge Henry McGinn.

Withycombe's office was flooded with letters and telegrams promoting other Republican hopefuls. Former senators Jonathan Bourne and Charles W. Fulton were both recommended on the basis of their experience. R. A. Booth of Eugene, who had been the Republican nominee for the Senate in 1914, also drew some support. But Booth had been shellacked by Democratic Senator George Chamberlain and Withycombe sought a nominee with broader appeal. Bourne and Fulton, though men of ability and intelligence, were considered shopworn and too old.

At 42, Judge McNary was regarded as one of Oregon's brightest young political figures. In addition, the governor and McNary shared a special bond as farmers and agricultural experimenters. For 16 years, Withycombe had been director of the experiment station at Oregon Agricultural College. McNary's development of the American filbert and the Imperial prune were recognized by Withycombe as considerable achievements. McNary's supporters made the argument that his appointment would be acceptable to both factions of the GOP and provide Republicans with the best chance of holding the Senate seat. "I know the appointment of some of the men suggested would be suicidal," wrote a Salem Republican. "I believe that the selection of Judge McNary would mean his re-election and continuance of the senatorship under Republican control."

Until the Governor approached him about the Senate appointment, McNary's political ambitions had been directed toward state affairs rather than Washington D. C. and he had some reservations about leaving Oregon for the nation's capital. He discussed his options into the wee hours with John in their law offices, which were on the third floor of the U. S. National Bank Building. When a Salem newspaper reporter saw the lights burning in the McNary offices at such a late hour, he filed a story predicting the judge's appointment.

John convinced his younger brother that it was an opportunity that could not be passed up. "Go on, Charley," said the elder McNary. "It'll be a nice experience and it won't last long." Charles said years later that he had accepted the appointment thinking that he would return to Salem after serving out Lane's unexpired term.

On 29 May 1917, Governor Withycombe announced McNary's appointment. "Judge McNary is splendidly equipped to fulfill the obligations and meet the opportunities of his position as United States senator," the governor declared.

The McNary appointment was well received. Oregon's newspapers were almost unanimous in their praise of Withycombe's choice. "A clean, honest, and upstanding citizen," said the *Portland Telegram*. The *Bend Bulletin* stated, "Charles L. McNary seems to fill the bill about as thoroughly as possible." The *Oregon Statesman* called McNary's appointment "the best that could have been made." Oregon's new senator, it predicted, "will serve every worthy interest of the state with ability and fidelity, and he will render patriotic aid to the nation in upholding its ideals."

After supporting McGinn for the nomination, the *Oregonian* described McNary as "a comparatively young man of excellent record and high character," noting that the new senator was a Republican "but his inclinations have been progressive and his acceptability to that element of the party doubtless greatly influenced the Governor in his favor."

Senator Chamberlain hailed McNary's appointment. "I have known Mr. McNary since we were boys and have every confidence in his ability and integrity," said Oregon's senior senator. "Governor Withycombe, I believe, has made no mistake. If a Republican must have the honor, I am willing to admit that the selection of Mr. McNary meets my entire approval."

Oregon's most popular Democrat, former Governor Oswald West, seemed elated by the appointment of his lifelong friend and predicted McNary would win a full term in 1918. At the time, West had been regarded as the probable Democratic Senate candidate but his fulsome praise of McNary was interpreted as a signal that he would not be running. "In placing the senatorial toga upon the shoulders of Charles L. McNary, the governor has acted wisely," said West, "for he is a young man of splendid ability, high ideals, and has always shown an earnest desire to render worthy public service."

Before leaving for Washington, McNary declared that he would strive to put principle above politics. "I am not a stand-patter," he said. "I am a progressive. Neither am I a hide-bound partisan. I shall support President Wilson in all of his progressive legislation. I shall stand behind him in all matters relating to our war with Germany."

McNary arrived in Washington D. C. in June 1917. As his train pulled into Union Station, Oregon's new senator saw factories along the tracks. From the station's pavillion and across the spacious plaza, he caught his first view of the grounds and the great dome of the Capitol. With the heavy scent of magnolias and the rows and rows of old brick buildings, Washington was distinctly a southern city. The Washington of 1917, though, was on the verge of great changes. Along Massachusetts Avenue, many stately palaces had been built by socially ambitious moguls of the industrial age. The homes were as flamboyant as the robber barons who lived in them. Now that America had entered the war, Washington was suddenly the mobilization center for manpower and industry. As a result, it was overcrowded. McNary and his wife took an apartment overlooking Farragut Square and just a block from the White House. From their livingroom window, they looked out over the well-manicured park that was dominated by a colossal bronze statue of Naval hero David Glasgow Farragut.

McNary's in the Senate Office Building was impressively furnished with a crystal chandelier and a dark mahogany desk. "I am allowed two stenographers at $1,200 each," McNary wrote a friend. "The Senate supplies the messengers and boys to do errands, aside from the clerical help supplied. These persons are placed on a salary and go upon the Senate roll and receive their money direct, whereas in the House the money goes to the Congressmen and in many instances he bargains for cheap hire." McNary was also entitled to an executive secretary at a salary of $2,000 annually. Portland editor Henry Hanzen had accepted the job with the understanding that it would be several months before he could come back to Washington.

"I have not had one minute for correspondence," McNary wrote Hanzen on 22 June. "I have had a lot of congratulatory letters and telegrams which had to be answered and many requests for official information which had to receive my immediate attention. When you arrive on the scene and become familiar with the work much of this will be off of my shoulders.

"I have had to look after the publicity end myself and attend to a thousand and one things a day which you know have kept me going at excess speed rate. I haven't time to write a long letter now but as the Senate took a 15-minute adjournment I thought I could take that time to write you briefly.

"I have no chairmanship and don't expect that I will have one this year, though I have been unusually well treated in the matter of committee assignments." McNary had been appointed to the committees on Commerce, Public Land, Railroads, Public Health, and Indian Affairs.

McNary soon cultivated a warm relationship with the Capitol Hill press corps. One of the most approachable members of the Senate, he spoke with a candor that was often disarming. He criticized other senators for spending little time on the floor and expressed disappointment that floor debate was so loosely structured. In one of his first Washington interviews, McNary was asked what interested him most. His reply was pure Frank Capra. "Nuts," said the young Oregon senator. On 1 July, a report in the *New York Morning Telegraph* said, "Although the Hon. Charles L. McNary of Oregon has been a member of the upper house of Congress for only three weeks, he fits into his place in that distinguished body with the ease of a man who has been a United States senator for at least one term of service."

On domestic issues, McNary identified with such western progressives as Norris of Nebraska, Robert La Follette of Wisconsin, and Hiram Johnson of California. Barely a month after his arrival, McNary introduced his first legislation, an amendment to the Wilson administration's flood-control bill that would provide twenty million for Western reclamation projects. "War necessities demand speedy action by the removal of all barriers to an abundant production," said McNary. "If we are to feed our people, and our armies and to assist in feeding our allies, we must look in part to those vast acres of unreclaimed lands that lie to the west, for there rests the potential possibilities of war's success." His amendment, McNary argued, would create millions of acres of food-producing farms on previously arid lands.

His amendment was defeated 42 to 29. It received almost unanimous support from the progressives—Norris, La Follette, Johnson, William Borah of Idaho, and Frank Kellogg of Minnesota. McNary's amendment was defeated by a coalition of Republican conservatives from industrial states and Democrats, including Senator Chamberlain. Handsome, silver-haired Warren Harding of Ohio had a well-deserved reputation as a profile in caution. After voting for the McNary amendment, Harding switched his vote to an abstention.

In the weeks ahead, McNary successfully lobbied for government purchase of such Oregon farm products as dehydrated potatoes, vegetables, and prunes.

He spoke out against war profiteers. "The consumer must be screened from the heartless exactions of the speculator," he declared. "No particular class must be made to feel the hardships of war while another class is permitted to enjoy the favor of its profits."

McNary introduced legislation that would have placed price controls on petroleum, leather, wool, livestock, farm products, and machinery. With other progressives, he contended that the war effort should be financed from industrial war profits. His legislation was defeated.

Interviewed in early August by the *Los Angeles Times*, McNary sounded downright radical. "Profit-sharing will become more general. Taxes on income will continue. Huge profits, as a consequence, will be discouraged. Inheritances will be more heavily taxed. Why should a father leave millions to his son or son-in-law to be spent in immoral or idiotic practices? Take a good part away from his estate, I say, and spend it for roads, schools and other useful purposes."

Though McNary and the progressive bloc failed to secure the restrictions on war profiteering in the summer of 1917, the dimensions of the problem became fully apparent by winter. Under congressional pressure, Wilson set up a War Industries

Board with sweeping powers. As its chairman, the president named Bernard Baruch, a Wall Street speculator, who performed masterfully in mobilizing the nation's industries.

Much to McNary's disappointment, Hanzen changed his mind about moving to Washington. In August, Hanzen wrote McNary that his efforts would be far more valuable in Oregon with the tough re-election campaign coming up, noting the expected challenge from Judge McGinn.

"I think your decision immature and made without much reflection," McNary answered. "By that I mean that you may be able to do me more good in Oregon during the next year, but what of the future providing I am successful in defeating my opponents be they few or many?

"Has this change of mind resulted from a fear of crushing defeat or do you feel the contest so close that your presence in Oregon is necessary for a proper administration of my political plans. Naturally you are much closer to the situation than I am, yet I am not disturbed over the candidacy of the gentleman whom you mention. One defeat has given me courage to withstand another and at the same time it has given me strength for battle."

No longer reluctant about staying in the Senate, McNary decided to fight for a full term. If he failed, McNary recognized that his political career would be over. It was a race he did not plan to lose.

In 1916 McNary managed the Oregon presidential campaign of Republican Charles Evan Hughes. Though Hughes was edged out by Woodrow Wilson, McNary delivered Oregon for his candidate. It was the only western state that Hughes carried. (Author's collection)

5

Triumph and Tragedy

RETURNING to Oregon in the fall, McNary resigned the state GOP chairmanship and announced that he would indeed be seeking a full Senate term in 1918. As the incumbent McNary possessed obvious advantages—influence over legislation, familiarity with national issues, and the ability to secure federal money for Oregon. On the other hand, he had yet to win an election. Beginning with his service as deputy district attorney, McNary had held public office by appointment and some critics suggested that his success had come too easily. Under such circumstances, a strong primary challenge was anticipated.

Much of the early speculation had focused on Judge Harry E. McGinn of Multnomah County, the *Oregonian's* favorite for the Senate. McGinn overcame a somewhat tainted past to become one of the state's leading GOP figures. There was doubt, however, whether McGinn's personal life could withstand the scrutiny of a statewide campaign. Although he was married, Judge McGinn frequented some of Portland's finest brothels and for years had been the companion of the notorious Madame P. Shong. In September, Judge McGinn discreetly took himself out of the Senate race and endorsed McNary. Former U. S. Senator Charles Fulton, disappointed that the governor had not named him to Lane's Senate seat, announced his candidacy for the Republican nomination. Soon afterward, Fulton suddenly died at the age of 64.

Oregon House Speaker Robert N. Stanfield emerged as McNary's leading challenger. At 40, Stanfield was tall, powerfully built, and handsome as a cowboy. His wealth and conservatism made him a favorite among the party's Old Guard. A veteran of many campaigns and three legislative sessions, he had a reputation as one of Oregon's best stump orators. Like McNary, he was of pioneer stock. Well before Oregon achieved statehood, Stanfield's father had settled in Umatilla County and established one of Oregon's first cattle ranches. Young Bob learned ranching firsthand and got his education from a country schoolhouse. In the often-heated disputes between the cattle raisers and sheep herders, he guarded the border of his father's ranch with a Winchester rifle to keep back advancing herders. As a result of his years in the saddle, Stanfield was bow-legged. Once Umatilla cattleman began turning over land to sheep herders, Stanfield switched to the sheep business. By 1918, he was said to be the largest sheep rancher in the world with 350,000 head. Stanfield made it known that he was prepared to spend any amount to win the Republican primary. A tough political infighter, Stanfield would give McNary an education in rough-and-tumble politics.

Before the end of the year, McNary named his brother John as campaign chairman and designated Portland real estate broker Thomas B. Neuhausen as campaign manager. Neuhausen, a shrewd political activist, had close ties to the state's progressive movement. The McNary brothers and Neuhausen planned their strategy for re-election. In a memorandum, the campaign manager advised the McNarys that Stanfield would have the support of the *Oregonian*, the state's biggest and most influential newspaper, and most of the Portland business establishment. Even so, Neuhausen pointed out that Stanfield was vulnerable to charges that he was anti-labor and a war profiteer as well. As a state representative, he had supported anti-picketing legislation, which could be contrasted with McNary's pro-labor judicial record. Neuhausen, noting that Stanfield had sold wool to the government at fat profit, urged McNary to step up his attack against war profiteering.

"Stanfield is going to open a vigorous campaign right after the first of the year," Neuhausen told John McNary in December. "Things have been brewing here on the quiet, there being a sort of gentlemen's agreement on the surface that until New Year's there would be an armistice, unless somebody shied the first brick. In the latter event, the air would be full of brickbats. The battle will soon be on."

In view of the war situation, McNary decided he should remain on the job rather than return for the campaign. America had just launched its major thrust on the Western Front. More than two million American troops would be deployed there in 1918 as General John J. Pershing moved to end the bloody stalemate. Wartime Washington was the nerve center of the American war effort and the government took unprecedented control of the national economy.

McNary's decision had been carefully calculated. "It is my present impression that we should not attempt to emulate that candidate whom gossip asserts will make a display and lavish expenditure," the senator wrote Neuhausen in January. "I believe attention to business and faithful service to the public will be of greater political potency."

The *Oregon Voter*, which supported Stanfield, charged that McNary was hiding behind his incumbency because he was a poor campaigner. McNary, it predicted, would "tire the audiences with windy recitals of his own good intent and still windier exhibitions of ignorance on subjects on which he speaks."

Without an active candidate, the resourceful Neuhausen pleaded with John McNary to make an appearance on the same platform with Stanfield at Medford's Lincoln Day dinner. The elder McNary, too, refused to campaign on the ground that it conflicted with his brother's strategy.

"When Charlie left for Washington, it was understood that he was going to his post of duty to remain until after the primaries," John wrote Neuhausen. "We then thought that the contrast between his work in Washington and Stanfield's traveling around the state in quest of votes would be favorable to Charles. When the meeting is called at Medford and Stanfield is there in person speaking and solicit [*sic*] votes and Charles' telegram from Washington is read, noting his absence in the interest of his constituents, the same matter will be called to the minds of the voters. This physiological effect would be beneficial to Charles' candidacy. Now my presence there would destroy that effect entirely for I would be there for no other purpose ostensibly than to solicit votes on my brother's behalf."

As in his earlier campaign, Senator McNary personally sent out hundreds of letters to friends asking for their support. This time, however, it was a much more sophisticated effort. Neuhausen, a pioneer of direct-mail political campaigns, utilized commercial mailing lists and voter rolls to distribute McNary letters, cards, and brochures. And, while Stanfield barnstormed the state, McNary appeared to be reaching more people. "For every man Stanfield sees," conceded the *Oregon Voter*, "there are two or three hearing from McNary directly in the most personal way or hearing from him indirectly through the Grange and other organizations."

McNary received strong organizational support from the Farmer's Union, the Grange, labor unions, remnants of the Progressive party, and the Non-Partisan League. His network of former law students provided many of the county chairmen. Henry Hanzen used the editorial columns of Portland's *Evening Telegram* in advancing McNary's candidacy and exposing Stanfield's wartime wool profits.

Acknowledging that he had done extensive business with the federal government, Stanfield contended that his motives had been patriotic. The *Oregonian* depicted him as a driving force in Portland's emergence as a national textile center. And the newspaper's editor, Edgar Piper, made campaign appearances for Stanfield. With his unlimited budget, Stanfield hired full-time campaign staffers in all 36 counties, stepped up his media campaign with newspaper ads and pamphlets, and sharpened his attacks on McNary. Stanfield charged McNary had been an ineffective senator and not even a loyal Republican.

"I shall say nothing with respect to any statement this fellow might make for the reason that when you step on a cockroach it only makes a mess on the floor," McNary wrote progressive ally George Rodgers. "If my eighteen hours of service here each day will not count against the statement of one so common as this fellow, I could say nothing that would supply me aid."

Stanfield's offensive troubled McNary's advisers and they urged the senator to reassess his passive strategy. "There is no question but that Stanfield is making headway throughout the state," John McNary reported on 23 March. "I think he has been gaining on us for the last month. By this, I do not mean that I think he will win, but I am satisfied that it will be necessary for us to exert all of our resources in order to be certain of success." The elder McNary added, "I do not believe you comprehend the character of the campaign that Stanfield is carrying on, or the amount of money that he has expended. I am satisfied that he has spent at least $50,000 to date." Attempting to change his candidate's mind about campaigning, Neuhausen wrote, "Your followers here are restless and becoming dispirited because they do not see any visible signs of tangible strength or progress in your campaign." McNary insisted it would be a mistake to rush home in response to the Stanfield attacks.

Another development did concern McNary. Former Governor West announced his candidacy for the Democratic nomination in April. Because of his friendship with McNary, West had previously indicated that he probably would not seek the Senate seat. Under pressure from the Wilson Administration, the former governor relented and agreed to run. Treasury Secretary William Gibbs McAdoo, Wilson's son-in-law, had personally appealed to West's party loyalty. The administration was counting heavily on retaining the Democratic majority in the Senate and West's entry into the race was considered their only hope of regaining the Oregon slot. As governor, West had been bold and innovative, winning the admiration of Wilson and Theodore Roosevelt.

Stanfield, capitalizing on the West-McNary connection, asserted that the senator was not a "100-percent Republican" but, rather, "a 50–50 Demo-Rep." The Republican challenger claimed that McNary had campaigned for West in 1910 against Republican Governor Jay Bowerman and received the Supreme Court appointment as his payoff. Stanfield further alleged that West gave Governor Withycombe his pledge not to run for the Senate if McNary got the appointment. The *Oregonian* highlighted Stanfield's swipes at McNary's GOP credentials and suggested editorially that West would withdraw in the event McNary won the primary.

John McNary finally spoke out when Stanfield questioned his brother's Republican credentials. "Much has been said during the last few days about 100 percent Republicanism and Charles L. McNary can measure up to that standard," he declared, "for he has been a lifelong Republican and a faithful worker in the Republican party. He has been a supporter of the candidates of the party ever since he was old enough to participate in campaigns and elections.

"Instead of returning to Oregon to conduct the campaign, my brother is remaining at his post of duty, and while he is serving his state and country in the Senate, I do not propose that Mr. Stanfield, or anyone else shall maliciously and falsely accuse him without being brought to account."

By repeatedly praising McNary, Democrat West reinforced Stanfield's charges. "His conduct seems to be to injure me among a certain class of Republicans," McNary wrote L. R. Webster. "If he had any regard for my interests, he would conduct himself very differently." Neuhausen felt West was doing everything possible to undermine McNary's candidacy in the belief Stanfield would be a more vulnerable opponent in the fall. Early in May, the wily and unpredictable West pulled another surprise with a proposal that all challengers in both parties withdraw in McNary's favor. The former governor commended McNary's support of the Wilson administration's war policies and said he deserved re-election. Stanfield said West's ploy was proof of McNary's Democratic leanings and stated that the senator's chances were "growing dim."

McNary fumed at West's audacious suggestion, telling friends the former governor was out to sabotage his re-election. Already suspect among the GOP's Old Guard, McNary felt West's action had made him appear even more an outsider. Yet he could not publicly accuse his old friend of Machiavellian motives, for West had been politically helpful to him. In a public statement, McNary repudiated West's proposal that his opponents abandon their candidacies. "I desire to say that Mr. West's proposal came to me as a complete surprise. Being a candidate, I am not made the confidant of my opponents for the senatorship in either party. What they do or may not do is entirely upon their initiative and not through any understanding with me. I have submitted my candidacy to the voters without reference to any other person's ambition and free from any notion or purpose that anyone should retire in my favor or make a political or personal sacrifice for me. Such a proposal does not command my sympathy."

Unwilling to drop the issue, Stanfield hammered away at McNary's ties with West. Stanfield's surrogate campaigners used Pier Six techniques in making slanderous comments about McNary's drinking habits and personal life. "Sewerish tales," McNary complained privately. Stanfield disclaimed responsibility for the free-swinging attacks but McNary put the blame on his opponent.

McNary's forces were not above using subterfuge. Seeking inside information about Stanfield's strategy in the campaign's final weeks, Neuhausen hired the Burns Detective Agency to infiltrate the campaign. With a generous expense account that included a daily allowance for liquor and cigars, Operative 174 easily worked his way into Stanfield's inner circle and began filing reports for his employers. The detective provided useful information about Stanfield's alliance with Portland Mayor George Baker, including plans to use the city's police department on election day "to whip the rooming houses, sporting elements, hotels, etc. into line." Several weeks after the investigator began leaking material to Neuhausen, he quoted Stanfield's manager as saying: "The McNary bunch seem to know just what is going on in our headquarters and we would like to know who it can be that is informing them."

In the last week of the primary campaign, Neuhausen called on McNary to "drop everything else" and line up some powerful endorsements for the stretch. "Conditions must be very bad," McNary told his brother, warning that such intervention by nationally prominent figures "might have appearance of outside influence." But the senator produced impressive blurbs from colleagues Borah of Idaho, Johnson of California, and Food Administrator Herbert Hoover.

Throughout the state, McNary's supporters indicated that he had surged ahead of Stanfield. "We want a Republican whom West cannot defeat and know Charlie McNary is the man," wired Benton County legislator A. J. Johnson. Medford city attorney Fred Mears added, "Republicans think this is no time to change and will retain Charles McNary, our war senator." A former McNary law student, George Neuner of Roseburg, predicted, "The 11th-hour mud slung at the man who is at his post in Washington will do him no harm."

John McNary, concerned about possible overconfidence, sent his brother's county chairmen election-eve telegrams warning them not to be too optimistic that they neglect to get out the largest possible vote.

On 17 May, Oregon voters went to the polls. From the earliest returns, McNary held a commanding lead on the strength of his showing in Portland and Salem. Neuhausen's detective reported voting fraud by Stanfield lieutenants in Portland. But McNary's lead was too wide to be threatened. In the end, the senator won 25 of Oregon's 36 counties, polling 52,546 votes to Stanfield's 30,999. West easily captured the Democratic nomination. At Stanfield headquarters, Portland's tobacco-chewing politicians were in agreement that McNary's strategy of remaining "at his post of duty" in wartime had made him unbeatable. Stanfield conceded gracefully, sending McNary a congratulatory wire, and promptly endorsing him.

For McNary, it was an enormously satisfying victory which brought him increased prestige in Washington and established him as the favorite to win another term. Although West was a formidable opponent, Republicans held a registration edge in Oregon of more than two-to-one. "I cannot adequately express to you my appreciation for the great work you performed for me during the last campaign," McNary wrote Henry Hanzen. "I attributed my tremendous majority in a large way to the efforts of you and John. I never felt at any time that there was a serious danger, because I was in a position to command the whole view and was in touch with every part of the state. Employing a word again which John does not particularly favor, the psychology of the public mind was right. Barnstorming politicians, rough necks, slanderers, political cockroaches and other denizens of the political zoos may howl, strut, bluster and fight, but they are not indicative of public sentiment nor do their little antics carry more than the weight of a bubble. The noisy politician stands in proportion to the public as a soldier does to the civilian population, and if you wanted to know the state of mind of the nation, you wouldn't cross the waters to inquire of a soldier, therefore, I believe that fellow who is in the thick of the fight sometimes places too much importance upon the noisy conflict made by the poignant politicians."

McNary had not planned to be in Oregon until the fall congressional recess. Jessie, however, returned to Salem following the death of her mother. On 3 July, she drove to Portland with her sister and brother-in-law, the R. P. Boises and met her other sister and her husband. Returning to Salem, the Boise car swerved to avoid hitting an oncoming vehicle about three miles south of Newberg. The car overturned, pinning Jessie underneath and she was instantly killed. The other passengers escaped with minor injuries. John McNary wired Senator Chamberlain and asked him to break the news to his brother.

It was the greatest blow of McNary's life. The years with Jessie had been so rich and fulfilling that it was impossible for him to imagine life without her. Leaving Washington's Union Station on the afternoon of 4 July, the senator was met in Portland four days later by John and Nina. Services for Jessie were held at the Breyman house in the same room where she had been married 16 years earlier. The statehouse was closed that afternoon in her memory. Long before the ceremony began the house was overflowing with friends and relatives. The floral displays included wreaths, ferns, and sweet peas. A huge spray of lilies and roses was sent by the Republican state central committee and another large spray came from McNary's Senate colleagues. It took two trucks to transport the flowers to City View Cemetery for graveside services. The pallbearers were all old friends— Ben Olcott, Phil Metschan, George Rodgers, T. C. Smith, Frank Lovell, and Henry Meyers. McNary's grief was deep and profound and would never fully heal.

McNary remained in Salem for a few days then returned to Washington and stayed there for the duration of the campaign. With the great outpouring of sympathy over his wife's death, McNary's lead over West in the Senate contest was probably unshakeable. The Republican senator was also receiving tacit support from the Wilson administration as a result of the president's feud with Senator Chamberlain, who, as chairman of the military affairs committee, had been sharply critical of Wilson's war leadership. Although Wilson's men had encouraged West to make the race, the president knew that the former Oregon governor was a Chamberlain protege and was skeptical of his pledge to support the administration. "I cannot do anything in his behalf," Wilson told political advisor Joseph Tumulty, "without condoning what I cannot condone on Senator Chamberlain's part." McNary, a proven commodity, had given Wilson unstinting support in the war.

West was scrambling. In another unorthodox proposal, he suggested that McNary join him in shutting down their campaign operations and letting the voters make their choice on the basis of their past records. "Your answer to West's suggestion," advised Neuhausen, "should be that the Republicans of Oregon honored you with the nomination because they wanted a Republican state to be represented by a loyal Republican and in consequence, it is your duty to do everything possible to be elected in November, so that the wishes of the Republican voters may be realized and while you desire and hope to retain the friendship of Mr. West, you are in honor bound to enter into no combination or agreement with him." McNary announced he would have nothing to do with West's proposal. The Republican state central committee had taken over McNary's campaign with Neuhausen and John continuing as his principal advisers.

Both political parties put moratoriums on campaigning until 19 October out of deference to the Liberty Loan drive. As the underdog, West came out swinging when he started campaigning in late October. The former governor was critical of McNary's Senate performance and claimed that only a Democrat could work effectively with the Wilson administration. Neuhausen counterattacked by publishing advertisements that quoted West's virtual endorsement of McNary the preceding spring.

From September to November, American forces were mounting their largest offensive of World War I and the very size of the thrust turned the balance of military power. American troops crushed the German salient at St. Mihiel and General Pershing took a million of his men into the Argonne Forest in a move to break the Hindenberg line. The Meuse-Argonne battle raged 47 days. On 1 November aided by British and French successes on the northern and central fronts, Pershing smashed through the German center and broke the Hindenberg Line which meant an Allied victory. Even before this breakthrough, President Wilson had been negotiating peace terms with Germany.

Wilson, fearing that he would lose prestige at the peace negotiations if Democrats failed to retain control of Congress, made a last-minute appeal to American voters for a show of confidence in his policies. "If you have approved of my leadership and wish me to continue to be your unembarrassed spokesman in affairs at home and abroad," Wilson declared, "I earnestly beg that you will express yourselves unmistakably to that effect by returning a Democratic majority to both the Senate and the House of Representatives."

In Oregon, West was hopeful that the president's appeal might salvage his candidacy. The Pendleton *East Oregonian* said the former governor would probably gain a significant silent vote following Wilson's speech. Wilson, however, had pointedly refused to give West an endorsement. And McNary's support of the administration had been well publicized. "Senator McNary has given the administration unqualified support in all war measures," noted an open letter to Oregon voters signed by Governor Withycombe, Supreme Court Chief Justice McBride, Stanfield, progressive leader William S. U'Ren, former Governor

48

Bowerman, and lumber mogul Simon Benson. "He is a statesman rather than a politician."

On November 5, Senator McNary received 54.2 percent of the vote, defeating West in all but two of Oregon's 36 counties, and polling 82,360 votes to 64,303 for the Democratic candidate. Portland lawyer Frederick Mulkey was elected for the remainder of Lane's unexpired term and resigned a month later so that the governor could reappoint McNary and give him a seniority advantage over other incoming senators. With the war at an end, McNary knew he would soon find himself more deeply involved in foreign affairs than ever before.

Henry Cabot Lodge, senator from Massachusetts and Wood-row Wilson's arch political rival, differed from McNary over the League of Nations. But Lodge soon became the Oregon senator's mentor and close friend. (Author's collection)

6

The League of Nations

SINCE COMING TO the Senate, McNary had been among the most outspoken Republican supporters of President Wilson's League of Nations, a world organization designed to prevent future international conflicts. In the summer of 1917, the *Los Angeles Times* listed him as one of "three or four Senate Republicans" backing the President's proposal. Former President William Howard Taft was the League's most prominent Republican advocate. Leading the opposition were Theodore Roosevelt and Senator Henry Cabot Lodge of Massachusetts, both of whom had previously looked with favor on the League concept but were determined not to let Wilson have any credit for it. "Mr. Wilson has no authority whatever to speak for the American people at this time," Roosevelt snorted as Wilson departed for the Versailles Peace Conference in December 1918. "His leadership has been emphatically repudiated by them. The newly elected Congress comes far nearer than Mr. Wilson to having a right to speak the purposes of the American people at this moment."

At the time, the former Rough Rider was widely considered the front-runner for the 1920 Republican presidential nomination. And if Roosevelt was the GOP nominee, the conventional wisdom was that Wilson would seek a third term. On January 6, 1919, the nation was jolted by Roosevelt's sudden and unexpected death at the age of 60.

Roosevelt is dead," McNary wrote Hanzen, "thus endeth the chapter of a busy life. The going of this good man has, in my opinion, simplified the political situation as it affects the Republican choice for the presidency. It may be said without provoking controversy that, if the National Convention had been held this winter, the Colonel would have been the leading candidate. His nomination would have visited upon the party political misfortune. In this connection I may add that the inner circle of Democrats longed to see the Colonel nominated; in fact would willingly have given him such publicity as his vanity demanded, upon the notion that Roosevelt running for a third term would counteract whatever censure which may have come to Mr. Wilson for running for the third term. In other words, no opposition at all could have been given Mr. Wilson while Roosevelt occupied a similar position, and it is believed by close friends of the President that he could defeat the former President in those states that are dangerously close."

Fully aware of Wilson's ambitions for another term, McNary argued that the League was beyond partisan considerations and should not be rejected in an effort to further Republican political fortunes. "Opposition to this notion simply because you cannot conceive of a structure that is totally perfect and capable of sheltering all the troubles that may arise among nations does not justify opposition," McNary wrote Hanzen, "and I am very much afraid that our party and some of our leaders are not looking into the hearts of the mothers of the country, nor feeling the mental pulse of the fathers. The candidate who excites sympathy for any movement which is designed to forever eliminate cruel wars has accomplished something that will attract public favor and support."

"The people of this country, as well as the people of other nations, are mad with the hope that this conflict has forever settled armed assaults. They are not particularly looking for something concrete, but they desire to know that their representatives are ever alert to use their influence towards some plan that is calculated to bring peace forever to the world. In fact, I go so far to say that a mere resolution and appeal to the conscience of men, yes, a prayer to the better instincts of humanity, will be esteemed with much more acceptance than a mere putting off of the issue because all cannot agree upon some perfect plan.

"So if we, as a party," McNary concluded, "take a position against the society of freedom from wars because we cannot agree upon the edifice to be constructed and with Mr. Wilson and his party cause to be inserted in the terms of peace, even though it must be left for the future to erect, then our party and the men who stood against the society will perish and democracy will have so firmly bent its roots into the national life of the country that it will take the storms of many decades to blot it from the secure position which it will have occupied in 1920."

Arriving in France, Wilson received greater acclaim from the cheering throngs than any Allied leader. The President was hailed as the peacemaker, the man whose intervention in the Great War had saved western democracy and whose visionary peace plan held the promise of averting future world wars. Wilson's Fourteen Point-Plan included an end to secret treaties, freedom of the seas, removal of trade barriers, armament reduction, breakup of the Turkish and Austro-Hungarian Empires with independence for each of the nations included in them, self-determination for the native peoples of European colonies, and, most importantly, the establishment of a League of Nations. Britain vetoed the "freedom of the seas" point and France's Clemenceau was unwilling to do away with secret treaties. Allied treaty makers punished Germany severely—stripping that country of its colonies, shrinking its borders, and saddling Germany with heavy indemnities. Wilson, holding that the terms were too vindictive, would not permit France to detach all of the Rhineland from Germany, nor would he allow Germany to be charged with the entire cost of the war. Finland, Poland, Yugoslavia, and Czechoslovakia were among the new states sanctioned under the Versailles Treaty. Though forced to accept many compromises, Wilson accepted them as a tradeoff for the League of Nations covenant.

Even before Wilson returned from Europe, his treaty came under attack in the Republican-controlled Senate. Thirty-nine senators signed Henry Cabot Lodge's petition objecting to the League of Nations "in the form now proposed" and urged that it be separated from the Versailles Treaty. McNary refused to have anything to do with the Lodge petition. Wilson, acknowledging that Lodge had the votes to block American entry into the League, went back to France and secured most of the changes in the covenant that the Republicans were demanding.

On 28 June 1919, the treaty was signed at Versailles. And, on 10 July, Wilson submitted it to the Senate.

The most vocal opposition came from the "irreconcilables"— Borah, Johnson, La Follette and thirteen other bitter-enders. A man of imposing presence, Senator William Borah was a dramatic orator who argued against any compromise on the League issue, pressuring Lodge into taking a harder line. Although Lodge was an internationalist who saw the United States as a world power he was motivated in the League debate by his strong dislike of Wilson. "I never expected to hate anyone in politics with the hatred I feel towards Wilson," Lodge confided in a 1915 letter to Theodore Roosevelt.

In McNary's view, Wilson had more than met the legitimate Senate reservations. "I have no objection to League opponents in the Senate being allowed to explain their construction or interpretation of the treaty," he declared, "but I certainly would object to any revision being attempted by the Senate that would materially change or nullify any portion of the document."

The Oregon senator conferred with Wilson at the White House on 18 July. Reviewing the Versailles Treaty, Wilson stressed the necessity for prompt Senate action. McNary said he and the president were in general agreement and reiterated his opposition to any amendment which endangered the League.

Four days later, McNary gave a speech in support of the League, urging his Republican colleagues not to play politics with so important an issue. "The issue created by the movement to combine nations to insure peace rises far above political platforms or party expediency. The subject, therefore, should receive that calm and just consideration made possible only when partisanship is adjourned. The quicker we forget our party affiliations the sooner will we be able to reach the proper solution of this tremedous problem."

McNary endorsed the controversial Article X under which member nations agreed to respect and defend against external aggression the territorial integrity of other member nations. "Indisputably this provision casts upon this country and every other member of the League a joint and several undertaking to go to war to protect an associate of the League from invasion through external force, but this obligation is in no proper sense a legal one, but purely a moral obligation, entirely dependent upon the condition that the cause of war and the war itself is violative of the moral conscience of the American people.

"This occasion is too serious for anger and recrimination, too big for partisanship, too full of good for personal considera- tion. Let this country be committed to a step in the direction of everlasting peace, and it is my sincere belief that the League of Nations is the greatest step the world has ever taken toward peace; therefore, I shall support the League, as it is the hope of the world."

It soon became apparent, though, that the Republican Senate would not approve the treaty without some alteration. McNary took the leadership of a group that would become known as the "mild reservationists," supporting the League covenant with relatively innocuous reservations. Other members of this bloc included Senators Frank Kellogg of Minnesota, Arthur Capper of Kansas, Irvine Lenroot of Wisconsin, and Albert Cummins of Iowa. Meeting at Kellogg's home in June, the group dis- cussed reservations that would protect national interests with- out undermining League principles or require further action by the other Allied nations.

Former President Taft submitted a draft of proposed reserva- tions to McNary and other pro-League Republican senators in the middle of July. Taft shared McNary's view that Article X should be left in effect so that the peace conference would not have to be reopened.

"I sincerely hope that early action may be had in the way of ratification of the treaty in order that the business of the world may be stabilized," McNary wrote Neuhausen in July. "It is my opinion that certain reservations may be agreed upon satisfac- tory to all except those who oppose the League on general principles."

Early in August, McNary and North Dakota Senator Porter McCumber introduced the McNary-McCumber reservations which recognized the Monroe Doctrine, endorsed a two-year withdrawal clause for member nations, and declared that Con- gress would retain its autonomy. The Oregon senator defined his reservations as "interpretative" rather than "amendments" which would have to be approved by other member nations. "By the avenue of reservations in the form of interpretation," argued McNary, "these questions could be placed beyond the pale of controversy."

McNary's efforts earned him the acclaim of such Democratic newspapers as the *New York Times* and *Oregon Journal* but were received with skepticism by GOP allies. "Some Republicans have grumbled because your attitude was interpreted by them as emphasizing President's insistence on making no changes in treaty," wired Neuhausen. "But if your group will now firmly insist on inclusion of essential reservations in ratification process resolution proper, entire situation will be clarified and correctness of your attitude from inception will be recognized and acknowledged."

"Believe a majority of Republicans will be found supporting reservations prepared by a small group of which I am a member," McNary replied. "Believe that Senate will compel early action irresponsible to attitude of Foreign Relations Committee; will adhere to plan that reservations be embodied in resolution of ratifications."

His optimism was premature. Rejecting any compromise, the president stormed out of the White House in September to begin a national speaking tour designed to rally public opinion behind his cause. For three weeks, Wilson barnstormed across the land. In the Far West, he was received as a conquering hero. "A League of Nations will not make war impossible," he declared, "but it will help to prevent future wars." Senators Borah and Johnson, meanwhile, took their crusade against the League on the road. McNary asked Neuhausen to help make the arrangements for Johnson's appearance in Portland. "Tho I do not agree with him on the League of Nations, and for that matter on other important subjects," McNary wrote, "I want the people of my state to hear both sides of the controversy. The Senator can present the opposition in an inimitable manner."

In Pueblo, Colorado, the President collapsed with terrible head pains, which were almost certainly the signs of a stroke. On his return to the White House, Wilson suffered a paralyzing stroke from which he would never recover. It would be months before his condition would become known to the American public. Though determined and courageous, Wilson was no longer capable of providing leadership in the most difficult political battle of his presidency.

On 10 September, the Senate Foreign Relations Committee submitted the treaty to the floor with a critical report that included four reservations and forty-five amendments. McNary and his mild reservationist brethren joined the Democrats in shooting down amendments that would have required reopening the peace conference. On 6 November, Senator Lodge presented the treaty with 14 reservations, the most important of which stated that Article X would not be binding unless Congress declared war. McNary had previously opposed tampering with the article which the president had called "the heart of the covenant," yet he decided that the League with the Lodge reservations would be preferable to a League without American membership. And it was becoming increasingly probable that the treaty would not pass without some reservations.

Reaching the same conclusion, Democratic senators pleaded with the ailing Wilson to accept Republican reservations. Most of the Wilson cabinet were in favor of a compromise. So, too, did his confidants Colonel Edward House, Joseph Tumulty, and Bernard Baruch. On 17 November, Senate Minority Leader Gilbert Hitchcock came to the White House and begged for a compromise. The senator was crestfallen when Wilson rejected anything short of complete acceptance. In a letter to Hitchcock, Wilson added, "I hope that all true friends of the treaty will refuse to support the Lodge reservations."

The Senate rejected American entry into the League on 19 November 1919, with Democrats opposing the treaty with Lodge's reservations and Republicans voting it down without the reservations. McNary voted for the Lodge reservations as the last hope for U.S. participation in the world organization. Wilson's stubborn refusal to compromise had resulted in the defeat of his ideal. On the evening of the treaty's rejection, champagne corks were popping at Alice Roosevelt Longworth's home and Lodge and Borah joined in the celebration. McNary blamed Wilson's intransigence for the treaty's failure. "I have no doubt that the treaty would have been ratified during the day that Congress adjourned had it not been for the President's letter to the Democratic members of the Senate," McNary ruefully commented.

When Congress reconvened the next month, the Oregon Republican continued seeking a compromise which would salvage the treaty. In 1937, Senator McNary confided to historian Thomas Bailey that he held in his safe-deposit box a copy of the democratic compromise resolution with revisions in Lodge's handwriting, including comments on Article X. (The McNary papers at the Library of Congress do contain this document with Lodge's writing.) In January of 1920, Lodge met with Democratic senators about breaking the deadlock over the

League. Lodge was forced to end the talks when Borah and the other bitter-enders threatened to oust him from the majority leadership if he persisted in his efforts. So Lodge never went public with another compromise.

Declaring that the League would lack authority without American membership, former British Foreign Secretary Viscount Grey suggested in late January that Britain would accept the Lodge reservations. The irreconcilables asserted that Grey's comments were proof of British influence over the League. McNary thought Grey had given new life to the pro-League forces. "I am encouraged by the statement made by Viscount Grey and by the statement the French minister made about ten days ago that it will be possible for us in this country to gather together and ratify the treaty with acceptable reservations," McNary told the *New York Times*.

Senator Lodge, however, would not make further concessions. And the President suggested that the 1920 elections would provide a national referendum on the League. On March 19, a majority of senators voted for the treaty with the Lodge reservations but the vote fell short of the requisite two-thirds. American membership in the League was permanently defeated.

Without U.S. participation, the League was much less than it might have been. Even so, there were considerable accomplishments. France and England provided leadership and direction on disarmament. Fridtjof Nansen, the Arctic explorer, served as the League's commissioner for refugees and earned a Nobel Prize. The League's peacekeeping authority was broken in the 1930s when Germany and Japan dropped out and its member nations did not respond to Italy's invasion of Ethiopia. Wilson felt that the United States had retreated into "sullen and selfish isolation."

Before the League debate, McNary had been an obscure young senator. His winning performance in a losing battle had impressed colleagues, who spoke of his fairness, nonpartisanship, and constructive efforts to salvage Wilson's treaty. Despite such personal recognition, McNary saw the treaty's setback as nothing less than a tragedy. "I shall never know whether it was the stubbornness of our distinguished President, Woodrow Wilson, the perversity of the able senior senator from Massachusetts, Mr. Lodge, or the eloquence of the irreconcilable senators that prevented the ratification of the Versailles Treaty," he told the *Oregonian* in 1922, "yet I shall always think, as a mild reservationist, that much of the unrest and hatred existing among nations at this time would not have occurred if this treaty containing the covenant of the League of Nations, with the Lodge reservations, had been ratified."

McNary on the U.S. Capitol steps during his involvement in the
League of Nations battle, 1919. (Author's collection)

7

The Harding Era

McNARY struck up a deep and lasting friendship with Senate Majority Leader Henry Cabot Lodge during the League of Nations debate. A generation older than the Oregon senator, Lodge took McNary under his wing. Even though the two men had differing views on the League, Senator Lodge felt that McNary had proven himself to be skillful and pragmatic in his efforts to reach a compromise that might salvage American entry into the world organization. Unlike the other western progressives, McNary had internationalist leanings and had demonstrated a willingness to compromise. In short, Lodge considered McNary a more practical politician than any of his western colleagues. Senator Lodge gave him an education in parliamentary skills, committee work, and the strengths and weaknesses of individual senators. A quick study, McNary soon became the chief link between Lodge and the western progressives. Lodge rewarded him with choice committee assignments, including Agriculture and a much-coveted slot as western member of the Committee on Committees. By the end of 1920, McNary had become part of the Senate's inner circle, a figure of rising influence. As chairman of the Irrigation and Reclamation Committee, he had a powerful voice in the development of the American West.

In the 1920 Republican presidential race, McNary stood with the progressives in backing California Senator Hiram Johnson. With McNary's support, Johnson narrowly edged General Leonard Wood in the Oregon primary. For all his differences with Johnson over foreign policy, McNary liked the California maverick and thought it would be politically helpful to have a president from the Far West. Senator Johnson went into the Chicago convention with more popular votes in the primaries and more pledged votes than any other candidate. The other contenders were General Wood, Theodore Roosevelt's commanding officer in the Spanish-American War and onetime Army chief of staff; and Illinois Governor Frank Lowden. The convention soon deadlocked and none of the major candidates would concede any ground.

Finally, on the tenth ballot, the Republican convention selected Senator Warren G. Harding of Ohio. Harding was chosen by a handful of political bosses in the notorious "smoke-filled room" in Chicago's Blackstone Hotel. In McNary's opinion, Harding was mediocre and unappealing, a throwback to the Gilded Age. Even so, McNary had regarded Harding as a possible choice for months. "He is cold, with a personality that is uninviting, the common run of men, inclined to be a little haughty," McNary wrote Hanzen in 1919, "with a legislative record that would be assailable from very many different quarters." McNary noted privately that the Ohio senator had voted with reactionaries "against many of the measures that were calculated to improve the social and economic conditions in this country.

"Their light shines from the rear, and in the history which extends from the present time back into the misty morning that bespeaks the coming of civilization they are very well versed," McNary wrote, "but of the light that shapes ahead a better world and citizenship they have not eyes to behold, and for that reason it would be easy, in my opinion, to find the vulnerable parts of their anatomy and thereby bring into play the subtle submarine that would sink their ambitions below the surface of the actions of men."

McNary's comments were restrained following Harding's nomination. "He is a conscientious worker, a person of deliberate judgment and his candidacy has met with popular response in all sections of the East." Senator Lodge and Harding's managers asked McNary to approach Senator Johnson and offer him the vice-presidential nomination. Had Johnson accepted, he would have become president within three years. But, at the time, Harding seemed ruddy and healthy and the vice-presidency held little appeal for Johnson. The California senator told McNary that he was not interested and the news was conveyed to Lodge.

As it happened, a lesser-known Oregon Republican, former Supreme Court Justice Wallace McCamant, emerged as the kingmaker. The party leaders had settled on Senator Irvine Lenroot of Wisconsin, a moderate progressive, as their vice-presidential choice. After Lenroot's name had been placed in nomination and seconded, Judge McCamant stood on a chair in the Oregon delegation, shouting for recognition. Frank Willis, presiding over the convention, recognized him, thinking that it was another second for Lenroot. But, the wiry, haggard-looking Oregon judge nominated Governor Calvin Coolidge of Massachusetts.

In a spontaneous uprising by the delegates, Governor Coolidge routed Senator Lenroot. Tired of boss control, the delegates were eager for a new face, a fresh personality and Coolidge became the man of the hour.

That fall, McNary campaigned for the Harding-Coolidge ticket. So did Hiram Johnson, Norris, Borah, Robert La Follette, Fiorello La Guardia, and Charles Evans Hughes. Harding was an image candidate whose golden voice and distinguished bearing gave him a statesmanlike aura. "He looked as a President of the United States should," wrote Frederick Lewis Allen. "He was superbly handsome. His face and carriage had a Washingtonian nobility and dignity, his eyes were benign; he photographed well and the pictures of him in rotogravure sections won him affection and respect."

After the stormy years of Wilson and Teddy Roosevelt, many Americans yearned for a return to calm and tranquility. Harding promised an era of "healing" and "normalcy." The Ohio Republican won the greatest victory in American history, crushing Democrat James Cox by a two-to-one ratio, and sweeping 37 of the 48 states. On the Pacific Coast, Harding carried every county and his coattails helped Republican Robert Stanfield, McNary's erstwhile rival, oust Democratic Senator George Chamberlain, which made McNary Oregon's senior senator.

Following the election, McNary sought a meeting with Harding. "If you want me to come and have an hour's session with you," wrote McNary, "I shall do so upon notification of the time, but if you think it unnecessary, as I do, I shall be happy to go over the field with you when you are nearer Washington than you are now." Harding invited him to St. Augustine, Florida, where he was vacationing, and McNary urged him to support western irrigation and reclamation projects. Harding, though friendly to the idea, gave no commitment.

In the winter of 1921, McNary became a charter member of the progressive, politically independent Senate coalition known as the "farm bloc." William Kenyon of Iowa was the group's leader and it included Norris, La Follette, Arthur Capper of Kansas, and Stanfield. McNary took pains not to burn his bridges with the Harding administration. When Harding opposed the Norris bill to resolve the farm surplus problem with an export financing corporation, McNary introduced the administration's substitute measure under which the War Finance Corporation extended credit to farmers. It passed and McNary termed it "the most helpful legislation to the farmers of the country and the people generally in many years."

McNary's legislative handiwork drew favorable reviews. The *Oregon Journal* reported. "The President is said to have expressed special regard for McNary's opinions in questions of agriculture, a regard that was no doubt enhanced when the Oregon senator took charge of the administration substitute for the Norris bill extending aid for agricultural exports."

McNary's most important ally within the new administration was Secretary of Agriculture Henry Cantwell Wallace. Prior to his appointment, Wallace had been one of the most admired farm leaders in the land as editor of *Wallace's Farmer*, an Iowa-based journal with a national readership. The Old Guard had fought Wallace's nomination because of his forthright editorials exposing the malpractices of meat packers and food processors. Harding, valuing Wallace's knowledge in farm matters, named him anyway. Though Harding considered the Senate farm bloc an insurgent movement and sought to undermine it, Secretary Wallace quietly worked with the progressives. McNary and Wallace became friends as well as allies. Once, when Harding sought to remove the farm bloc's leader, Senator Kenyon, by naming him to a federal judgeship, Wallace privately urged Kenyon to stay on Capitol Hill. Early in 1922, Harding sweetened the offer and Kenyon became a judge on the U.S. Court of Appeals.

President Harding also approached McNary about the U.S. Court of Appeals, but the Oregon Republican declined. Later, when John McNary suggested that his brother might consider leaving the Senate for the federal bench, Charles replied, "Why should I take a place like that when I told the President that I would not occupy a position on the Court of Appeals? Why should I retire to the robed sanctuary? Heavens, haven't I done enough cruel work in confinement, been driven like a quarry slave to his dungeon? Defeat, it hath no sting, success, it hath no victory.

I would rather take defeat than to accept a job on the district federal bench," McNary said. "My God, what a position, trying bootleggers and fining drunken Indians, calling to order lawyers for the slums while defending dope fiends, working like a slave—for what—barely a living wage."

The main reason that McNary had no aspirations for the federal bench was that his power and influence in the Senate were continuing to grow, helped in no small part by Senator Lodge. "I went to Senator Lodge's home last night," he wrote John in July of 1922. "I am taken in on all the inside movements now." A few weeks later, McNary added, "I have grown quite close to the old man during the last year and go to his house frequently for conferences." Lodge now had McNary assisting him with leadership duties on the floor. When progressives sought better committee assignments, it was McNary whom they asked to make their case before Lodge. "I am enjoying my work here tho it has grown to great proportions," Charles reported in March of 1922. "I have a very good place in the Senate now and within the last year have attained a position of considerable influence, due to a knowledge of the subjects of legislation, as well as to hard work, and particularly to positions on committees."

In 1922, McNary was named chairman of the Agriculture Subcommittee charged with reporting the administration's annual agriculture bill. He also served as chairman of a joint subcommittee on farm appropriations. That summer, Senator Norris offered to step down as chairman of the full Agriculture Committee in McNary's favor.

"He talked to me before he left for the summer a day or two ago," McNary wrote his brother in July. "I begged him to hang on. I want to get my reclamation bill through while I am chairman of that committee. Of course, eventually, I want to get hold of the Agricultural Committee, which, in times of peace, is one of the three highest committees of the Senate. It covers, of course, a tremendous subject, operating in every state of the Union, and if I get the chairmanship of it, I will be the first man from the West who ever had it, and will have obtained it quicker than anyone. Fortune attended me in my scramble from the bottom of the committee. Death and defeat thinned the ranks, and as a member of the Committee of Committees, I let no opportunity pass whereby my position could be advanced."

At McNary's urging, Senator Norris remained as committee chairman. The Oregon senator backed Norris's ambitious plan for public development of Muscle Shoals on the Tennessee River. And, with Norris, McNary fought to block the government from turning over the Tennessee Valley dams to private industry. Eventually, McNary was hopeful that the vast hydroelectric potential of the Columbia could be harnessed and utilized for public distribution.

Though never an insurgent, McNary maintained his progressive credentials in opposing the Harding administration on selective issues. In 1921 he voted against Harding's treaty to pay Colombia for the United States' seizure of the Canal Zone and supported Borah's amendment absolving the United States of responsibility for the secession of Panama. McNary supported a soldiers' bonus against administration opposition and voted to override the president's veto of the measure. He was critical of Treasury Secretary Andrew Mellon, whom he pronounced a "Croesus of Wealth." In December of 1922, McNary was one of nine senators invited by La Follette to plan progressive strategy.

McNary's independence was tempered with pragmatism. As a Republican senator in the Harding era, he strove to remain on good terms with the president. He was the administration's chief sponsor on major farm bills. He backed Harding's proposal for American membership on the World Court. He sided with Harding in the Senate battle over the seating of Michigan's Truman Newberry. In his 1918 Senate campaign, Newberry had spent more than $200,000. Following the election, the Michigan senator and 133 contributors were convicted of fraud, conspiracy, and corruption. In 1921, the Supreme Court overturned the conviction. Nine GOP progressives, contending that Newberry had bought the election, moved to bar him from the Senate. The president, a golfing companion and Newberry crony, threw his support and prestige behind the Michigan Republican.

John McNary, noting the public outcry against "Newberryism," told his brother that he had committed a major blunder in voting to retain the Michigan senator. The elder McNary called it the most unpopular vote of his brother's public career. "I have no doubt of that statement," Charles answered on 21 January 1922. "I had full knowledge of it before I shaped my course, but I did what I thought was right in the matter and will uncomplainingly submit to such punishment as it is metered out to me. In my now approaching five years service, I have found that conscience is the only guide and that public opinion is to be forgotten in regard to legislation. It is easy to jump on $200,000 and expenditures of that sum or any similar sum are indefensible."

A compelling factor in his Newberry vote, McNary admitted, was keeping on friendly terms with the White House. "If I am to be of influence here," he told John, "I can't be chasing with the Democrats and anti-administration Republicans every few minutes because of a rabid press abuses somebody or some specie of legislation. If the people of Oregon would have me sit out on the end of a limb and vote for me just for that reason, then certainly, public service with me is ended." He wrote a Salem friend, Louis Lachmund: "You have to go along with the administration some time if you want to be a part of it."

McNary had reason to be relieved that he was not up for re-election in 1922. Seven pro-Newberry Republicans lost their Senate seats and their defeats were linked to the controversial vote. Soon after the election, Newberry resigned. McNary expressed private concern that the issue would haunt him in the 1924 elections.

The Oregon senator disapproved of the Harding administration's record on conservation and the handling of natural resources. Under Albert Fall, the Interior Department seemed all too eager to open up public lands for private developers. Fall made no secret of his intentions. He wanted to gut federal conservation programs and make public holdings available to wealthy interests. A former New Mexico senator, Fall had been a poker-playing crony of Harding's for years. His chief qualification for the cabinet was that the President liked him. Early in the Harding presidency, McNary began picking up rumors about a corrupt alliance between Fall and oil companies. In 1921, at Fall's request, Harding signed an executive order transferring oil reserves at Elk Hills, California and Teapot Dome, Wyoming from the Navy Department to the Interior Department, which leased them to a pair of wealthy oilmen.

It struck McNary as a giveaway of public property. And he immediately protested to Harding and Fall. Even more disturbing to McNary were reports that Fall was set to go on the payroll of Harry Sinclair, one of the Teapot Dome oil moguls. In a 2 February 1924 letter to his brother, McNary recalled: "There is a little unwritten history in connection with this matter which I shall not tell because I am not seeking notoriety, but I went to see Mr. Fall and protested against disposal of the naval leases, upon the theory that Congress was wise when it had set these great oil properties aside for future use of the Navy. I made the same statement to Warren Harding, and further stated to my dear old friend, that if Mr. Fall went into the employ of the Sinclairs, after giving them Teapot Dome, that a national scandal would follow."

Harding did not publicize Fall's looting of the public domain. But his attitude toward the bombastic and cynical Interior Secretary had definitely cooled. In this crisis—which would become one of the most infamous political scandals in the nation's history—Harding asked McNary to replace Fall and provide new leadership at the Interior. On 3 January 1922, McNary wrote his brother: "A delegation called me yesterday, including Senator Watson who had come from a conference with the President, and offered me the position of Secretary of the Interior, commencing March 4th, but I would not have the job at any price. I would rather take Weathers' place at the farm, driving the tractor in season and chawing tobacco in rainy days in the winter." McNary once again refused to give up his Senate seat and in future years would turn down other offers of cabinet portfolios. When McNary turned Harding down, Postmaster General Hubert Work was tapped as Fall's replacement.

By the late spring of 1923, Harding was deeply upset by revelations of widespread graft and corruption in the Justice Department and Veterans Bureau. His political associations and friendships had left his presidency seriously tarnished. "I have no trouble with my enemies," Harding told William Allen White, "but my damned friends, they're the ones that keep me walking the floor nights." On a journey to the West Coast via such cities as Portland, Oregon, Harding looked pale and tired. Then, on 2 August 1923, he died of a heart attack in San Francisco. The nation grieved but the worst scandals of the Harding era had not yet become public knowledge. History would remember Harding as the worst of all American presidents.

McNary's warnings about Teapot Dome were indeed prophetic. A Senate investigating committee led by Thomas Walsh of Montana revealed that Fall had taken a $100,000 bribe for the naval oil leases. Fall would become the first cabinet member sent to prison for a felony committed while in office. The former Interior Secretary claimed that the payments had been "loans." Following his resignation, Fall had gone to work for Sinclair. McNary was appalled that Fall would not admit his guilt. "He fell and in his falling, he dashed himself to pieces," McNary wrote Lachmund. "Again, I recall one peculiarity of temperment. He often boasted of his bravado and a number of Mexican ruffians that he had shot to death, but when he got into a tight place covering moral turpitude, he did not have the moral courage and cringed like a quarry slave scourged to his dungeon. A more timorous man would have acted with more courage. And again we find that the dog that bays the moon is usually the one who kills the sheep."

McNary pressed for the resignation of Navy Secretary Edwin Denby, citing his misconduct in office that had culminated in the oil giveaway. Back home, McNary's efforts to remove Denby were criticized by the Republican Old Guard. "If politics has reached such a low ebb that I must take into my vote consideration of politics, then I want to retire," he wrote John. "The hyenas that are telling are a bunch of reactionary crabs that never were my friends and are using this vote as a screen to hide their envy and dislike for me. I shall not vote for crooks to hold office, and can't understand how any man can try to defend this old fellow Denby."

One week after the Senate passed a resolution calling for his resignation, Denby quit the cabinet. "Denby steps out of the Cabinet on March 10th," McNary wrote, "an admission of his wickedness and unfitness and the necessity of his retirement." In a letter to Lachmund, McNary added, "There has been some grumbling over my Denby vote, but I think his resignation and subsequent events have vindicated my vote. I did the thing that all wanted to do, but not all had the courage to do. I have not cast one vote yet where I considered politics as a factor in making my decision, nor shall I. If that is the test of service, then I am committed to the farm."

McNary's re-election in 1924 was far from certain. A powerful and sinister new force had emerged in Oregon politics and its hooded leaders were committed to McNary's destruction.

McNary at fifty. This portrait, which was taken on the steps of the U.S. Capitol, was widely used in his 1924 re-election campaign. (Author's collection)

8

Invisible Empire

"WE WOKE UP one morning and found that the Klan had about gained control of the state," Oregon Governor Ben Olcott declared at the 1922 National Governors Conference. "Practically not a word had been raised against them." While the Ku Klux Klan of Reconstruction had been a Southern phenomenon, the revived Klan was a national movement, which had capitalized on the postwar wave of ethnic hatred. Under the banner of "100 percent Americanism," the Klan had caught on in rural districts and small towns where Protestants felt threatened by the encroachment of "foreigners" and the alleged evils of big cities. Outside the South, Catholics were the main target of Klan abuse although Jews and blacks were also intimidated. By using modern promotion techniques, the Klan had enrolled a national membership of four million by the spring of 1924. The *New Republic* reported that the "Invisible Empire" now dominated the politics of Indiana, Texas, Oklahoma, and Arkansas—and held major influence in Ohio, New Jersey, Maine, Connecticut, and Oregon.

In McNary's home state, ambitious politicians were flocking to get their white uniforms. Carrying American flags and flaming crosses, white-sheeted Klansmen marched at the state fairgrounds on Armistice Day in November of 1921. On a hillside near Medford, the Klan burned crosses and hung two black men in "practice" lynchings. The Klan prevented the opening of a Newman Club on the University of Oregon campus. Klan members were elected city officials in Astoria, Tillamook, and Eugene. In Multnomah County, two Klansmen were elected county commissioners.

Governor Olcott was among the few Oregon political leaders who courageously spoke out against the secret society. In the 1922 Republican gubernatorial primary, Olcott's bid for renomination was challenged by State Senator Charles Hall of Coos County, the Klan's candidate. On the eve of the primary, the governor attacked the Klan for "stirring up fanaticism, race hatred, religious prejudices and all of those evil influences which tend toward factional strife and civil terror." By less than a percentage point, Olcott squeaked past Senator Hall to win the primary. The Democratic nominee, Walter M. Pierce, obtained the Klan's support in the general election by endorsing a ballot measure outlawing parochial schools in Oregon. As a result, Pierce was rated a good bet to overcome the two-to-one GOP registration advantage and defeat the Republican governor. McNary's friends urged him to stay out of the campaign and avoid the Klan's wrath in his 1924 re-election bid. Yet the senator abhorred the invisible empire and its growing influence in his native state.

Acknowledging the possibility of Klan reprisals, McNary told John soon after the primary that he wanted to help Olcott. "It appears to me at this time that I must meet the issue that was raised by the Governor," he wrote on 7 June. "I will then have to deplore the present situation. Then, of course, I will be marked for slaughter, should I become a candidate. And, in the contest, fanaticism takes no heed of prestige, position or devotion to duty. I am against the principle of mixing religion with politics, and would not be willing to become the candidate of any religious class. I am not afraid to run for this office upon the position I have here in the Senate."

The Senator's brother argued that it would be politically unwise to campaign for Olcott and advised him to stay in Washington. "God forbid that it ever gets any worse than you depict in your letter," McNary replied on 27 June. "Against this mob of fanaticism, character, purpose, industry, success, mean nothing. Hell is springtime compared with this terrible winter in politics. The hardest blow of all was the request that I remain banished from my native state until after the election. That is a high price to pay for politics, when you are anxious to see the folks at home. I suppose, as an abstract proposition in politics, it would be a good thing. Then I could do it easily, because of committee work, so that it would not at all be noticed."

Oregonian editor Edgar B. Piper traveled east in June and warned McNary to stay out of the Oregon campaign. "He [Piper] said that he felt I was tremedously strong throughout the state and admonished me, the same as you, that the pitfall was the religious situation in Oregon," Charles reported to his brother. "He said that I should do everything possible to keep out of it. Good advice, but darn hard to do if I am on the ground, as I am expected to go to bat for the ticket, including the Governor, as soon as I return to the West. Then of course, I am considered for the Governor and would become the target of the K's. Darn such a situation!"

Throughout the long summer of 1922, John McNary kept his brother appraised of the Oregon political situation and continued to insist that the senator keep his distance. "I suppose I must obey my brother," McNary wrote in August, "but I will be damned if I will ever be exiled again for any office on this planet. It is a dirty shame that politics has reached the state where a man cannot touch it without getting his eyelashes burned."

McNary made tentative plans to spend most of October in Europe on a legislative junket. Officially, the purpose of his trip was to study European farm-insurance plans but Oregon Republican leaders were not fooled. Congressman Clifton N. McArthur of Portland, another Klan target, called on McNary to take a stand. Under such conditions, McNary knew what he had to do. "I don't want the fellows at home to say that I would not do anything for the state ticket, the state organization or the party, and that through personal cowardice, I remained away," he wrote his brother on 2 October. "I would rather go out there and make several political speeches to show that I am not afraid."

Returning to Oregon, McNary fought prejudice squarely and condemned the Klan. In Astoria, he spoke in Olcott's behalf and the Klan repeatedly disrupted his speech by ringing an alarm bell under his platform. "I was under such a nervous strain," McNary wrote.

The senator's intervention could not save Governor Olcott and McArthur. Pierce won the governorship by the greatest vote ever received in an Oregon gubernatorial election. By a smaller margin, the Klan's compulsory public-school bill was approved by Oregon voters and Mississippi-born Democrat Elton Watkins, supported by the Klan, unseated Congressman McArthur. The

Klan claimed that it now controlled the Oregon legislature. More than a few political observers said that McNary was vulnerable to a Klan challenge two years hence.

McNary, sensing that he was in trouble, buckled under Klan pressure and withdrew his candidate for United States attorney in the Oregon district. For McNary, it was an extremely distasteful and uncomfortable episode. In yielding to expediency, McNary deeply hurt a man whom he had considered one of his closest friends. George Neuner of Roseburg had been McNary's original choice for the post. Neuner, then district attorney of Douglas county, had been a member of McNary's first graduating law class at Willamette. "Our relations have always been cordial," McNary said, "and of course, he looks back to the time when I was the Daddy of the Law School and he was one of the children, and really this feeling is mutual with me." In each of McNary's political campaigns, Neuner had served as Douglas County chairman. A successful politician in his own right, Neuner had been Roseburg's city attorney and had served in both houses of the Oregon legislature before becoming Douglas County's prosecutor. In the spring of 1922, McNary was set to name his protege as U.S. attorney, telling his brother that Neuner was "the most logical candidate" and met the geographical requirement that the appointment be given to a downstate lawyer. John cautioned the senator that the appointment would be political dynamite because Neuner's German immigrant parents had been Catholic.

"Should I retract," McNary replied, "then it would appear that it was through fear of the K's and it would then be said that I was controlled by the K's and control is quite as bad as membership."

Soon after the 1922 Oregon primaries, McNary informed the Justice Department that he would delay appointment of a new federal prosecutor until the end of the year. "No one foresaw the rising flood of fanaticism, nor did I know of his faith, nor did I consider it," McNary wrote John on 27 June. "If I have got to turn down everybody, because they are not of the Klan, I am out of the game of politics."

Puzzled about what had stalled his appointment, Neuner confronted McNary in Washington. When the senator told him, Neuner confirmed that his parents were Catholics but that he was not. Neuner had married a Presbyterian, Myrtle Campbell, and their children were being reared in the Protestant faith

"He spoke about the K's very plainly," McNary wrote his brother on 17 July. "It will be a darn shame if I can't appoint George as you know what our relations have been since he attended the Willamette College of Law when I was Dean. He is a fighter and looked after my welfare in Oregon some years ago. He is a hundred percent loyal, and to think that a lot of darn cranks who ought to be put in confinement, can prevent an appointment of this character, makes me sick. I rest on the future and of course will make no commitment until I discuss it with you."

John McNary told his brother to withdraw the Neuner appointment. And, in the wake of Governor Olcott's defeat and the Klan sweep, Senator McNary opted for minimum-risk politics and dropped Neuner. In his place, the Oregon Republican nominated Judge James L. Coke of Marshfield. Embittered, Neuner scolded his former mentor in a stern note. "I was disappointed with the fellow," McNary confided to John.

"Lord only knows," McNary wrote, "I hated to do as I did. It is impossible to play politics in Oregon. There is an awful bunch of peculiar people there, worse than in any state in the Union, in my opinion. They seem to lie awake nights fixing up jobs and digging pitfalls for a poor devil who is working like a dog at this end, and getting along very well. But doing rather large things is not comparable to putting up a K.K. job on a fellow between two and three a.m. when the night is dark, and spooks are slipping down the dim alleys. But I will stay in the game for a little while, and G.D. 'em, they have not got me licked until the polls are closed."

When McNary bowed to expediency, Oregon Attorney General I.H. Van Winkle named George Neuner as his chief deputy.

Meanwhile, the Oregon senator was agonizing over whether to seek another term. For more than a year, he had been privately suggesting that he might retire in 1924. "Now let it be known that I am not going to make a house to house canvas to hold this job," he wrote his brother in February of 1922. "Far be it from me to make a begging campaign. Furthermore let me say that I do not covet this job as a saint covets a heavenly home. I have been here nearly six years, and during that time I have been kicked about and look very much like a football that has served a season in an Indian training school. And, just as you say, the people do not care if I answer every roll call, act independently on every vote, work from early in the morning until late at night, nor whether I stand high or low in the Senate. It is what the fanatics think, and from the tone of your letter, they would seem to be greatly in the majority in Oregon, so what's the use.

"Frankly I don't know that I shall become a candidate again," McNary wrote in March of 1922. "I would not in the face of considerable opposition, because the position is not worth the price. . . . Of course, I do not desire to return to the practice of law, so the only thing I could do is to farm. Whether I would be content to leave a life of action, and take up one that is seasonable and sometimes dull, and be happy, I am in doubt."

For all his complaints about the ordeals of political life, McNary could think of nothing else that he would rather do. He had already turned down a cabinet appointment and the U.S. Court of Appeals. His most recent opportunity had been a partnership in a top Washington law firm. "I have had a splendid offer to go with a law firm in Washington," he told his brother. "Might possibly consider it but if I did not sit tight in this game at this time they would think I was afraid and there is no such thing as that in my makeup."

In the face of Klan opposition, McNary was determined to seek re-election. "The public mind is still dislocated," he wrote John on 6 February 1923, "and added to that unfortunate condition, bigotry, superstition, and hatred make the situation nebulous. I am doing the best I can, and if that is not satisfactory, then I will go down to defeat smiling, and without regret."

Uneasy about his brother's 1924 prospects, John suggested in April of 1923 that Charles take up President Harding on his earlier offer of a federal judgeship. "I wondered if you wanted me to withdraw for fear of my defeat in the next primaries," the senator replied.

"I am not half as disturbed over the political situation as the fuming, fretting, foaming politicians that crown the Imperial Hotel and the Arlington Club. I was advised by friends all through the Stanfield contest that I had no show." The senator was less worried about the Klan than his brother. "I think the K.K.K.'s are on the wane," he observed.

Announcing his candidacy for re-election in November of 1923, McNary denounced racial and religious prejudice and called for upholding civil liberties and freedom of religion. "Other candidates may seek to further inflame existing animosities by appeal to racial and religious prejudices in the belief that such a course will reap a harvest of vote, but I shall not do so.

"I am unalterably opposed to the injection of racial or religious issues into politics, no matter what the source. I believe the people of Oregon desire this campaign among the candidates be submitted upon issues involving national welfare, federal aid for and governmental cooperation with the state, and not upon a subject expressly removed from politics by our federal and state constitutions.

"I therefore offer my candidacy as one who has endeavored to work in the interest of, and without discrimination to all classes and creeds. I shall neither solicit nor seek the endorsement of any organization, group, clique or faction whose principles or doctrine contravenes either the letter or spirit of our constitution and laws."

In the meantime, McNary's Republican rivals were courting Klan support. Fred Gifford, Oregon's Grand Dragon of the Invisible Empire, Knights of the Ku Klux Klan, plotted his campaign strategy in his Pittock Block office in downtown Portland. There was no shortage of candidates eager for Gifford's endorsement.

Portland Mayor George L. Baker was a formidable opponent. In March of 1923 the mayor had given an eloquent testimonial to Gifford at a Klan banquet in a thinly veiled bid for his blessing in the GOP Senate race. Darkly handsome and an indefatigable campaigner, Mayor Baker was a masterful urban politician who had elevated patronage to an art form. Working his way up from newsboy and bootblack to Portland's leading theater owner, Baker was a Horatio Alger character sprung to life.

Fifty-seven years old in 1924, Baker was a political veteran who had won a seat on Portland's city council in 1898, and was elected mayor in 1917 two months after the United States went to war. A flamboyant showman, Baker was renowned for his emotional speeches before patriotic audiences. With moist eyes, he presided over breakfasts in the Civic Auditorium for every group of Oregon soldiers before they embarked overseas. Baker richly enjoyed leading the Rose Parade and sharing the spotlight with visiting celebrities. *Oregonian* photographer Frank Sterrett described him as "the biggest ham in town." During the Red Scare, Mayor Baker was brutal in crushing the Wobblies and other radical groups. Baker struck his alliance with the Klan in December 1921 when he gave police authority to 100 vigilantes, mostly Klansmen. Although Baker denied that he was a member of the hooded order, former Klan editor Lem Dever disclosed that the mayor was a full-fledged Klansman.

Also vying for Klan support against McNary was Oregon House Speaker Kaspar K. Kubli who had proudly accepted a free membership in the Portland chapter of the Klan because of his initials. Speaker Kubli recruited other state legislators to join the Klan and initiations were held behind closed doors in the Oregon statehouse. Until the Klan's breakthrough in the 1922 elections, Kubli was best known as the legislature's most strident red-baiter. He had co-sponsored the most repressive anti-radical legislation during the Red Scare years. A native of Jacksonville, Kubli graduated from the University of Oregon and Harvard Law School, then went into the printing business in Portland. In his Senate campaign, Kubli was advocating a national law that would outlaw all parochial schools, just as Oregon had done.

The Klan faced a political dilemma. In some states, the invisible order held its own primaries to determine which candidates to support in statewide elections. Both Baker and Kubli were running hard for the Klan's official endorsement. Most of the local Klans were supporting Kubli whose campaign literature was anti-Catholic propaganda. Lem Dever, editor of *Western American*, the Klan's official newspaper, threw his support behind Kubli. Fred Gifford, titular head of the Oregon Klan, endorsed Mayor Baker but was unable to convince many of the local Klans to switch from Kubli. With this division, the Klan suddenly seemed much less of a threat to McNary's renomination.

McNary, who had regarded Kubli as a stalking horse for Baker, was encouraged by reports of the state legislator's success in pursuing Klan support. "I believe the endorsement of the Klan for Kubli would have been a good thing and will be if it goes over in March," he wrote his brother in February. "It seems that he has been endorsed by most of the local Klans, therefore give him the Klan vote; but those who oppose the Klan only look to the large power and that is the state endorsement."

The senator was plainly unhappy with rumors that Gifford was reassessing his support of Baker and might instead back him for re-election. "The continuous report that there is an understanding between me and Gifford is absurd beyond argument," McNary wrote John on 4 February, "but it certainly is doing me no good, and I would predict some damage." Several days later, McNary asked his brother not to be concerned by the Klan's "men of mendacity." He added, "For seven years, I have been abused and lied about and while I have not become used to the slander of scoundrels, you must necessarily let it pass you as an idle wind that you list not."

For the Klan to unseat him in the primary, McNary said they would have to come up with another candidate who could cut into his downstate strength. "I have long thought that my opposition would like to have another Valley man to scatter my vote, and I have long thought that they would get Kubli out of the race, giving Baker a clean field in Multnomah County, and transferring the money that might be used for Kubli to Seymour Jones or some other gink that lives outside of Multnomah. I believe this to be good politics from the standpoint of my opponents."

Despite intense pressure, Kubli would not pull out of the Republican contest, vowing to fight McNary down to the final bell. The state legislator's chances, however, had all but vanished. As his prospects faded, Kubli's rhetoric became even more shrill and inflammatory. "Education and immigration are the two greatest problems that concern our nation," stated Kubli. "We should have a free, universal and unifying compulsory system of education in order to assimilate, Americanize and maintain intact our American nationality." Both Kubli and Baker called for restrictive immigration and "Americanizing" the "alien population."

Mayor Baker could not be lightly regarded. "Now I assume that I have a real fight on," McNary wrote John on 1 April, "and I further assume that the result is uncertain, but these two factors are not so predominant that I should return to Oregon the last few weeks of the campaign."

Taking the offensive, Baker took his senatorial campaign downstate and ridiculed McNary as an ineffective legislator. To a friend, McNary wrote of the mayor's slam-bang attack: "I read it with amusement and wondered if a harangue of that kind would influence any votes. Of course I have opposition in Salem, that is natural and indeed to be expected, but I think the opposition to me would carry votes for Baker rather than his speech."

79

Alerted that his campaign treasury was running dry, McNary told his brother that he would not "beg" for contributions. When it was pointed out that Mayor Baker was twisting arms with Portland businessmen and raising a huge campaign fund, the senator was unmoved.

"Now the truth of the matter is, in my judgment, that ninety cents out of every dollar is wasted in a campaign," McNary responded. "The name of McNary and what it stands for is known up and down the valley. I can't conceive how a whole lot of money is going to help one bit. . . . If I can't win on a $2,500 campaign, I can't win, and I don't want to win and I shouldn't win. And if defeated by reason of not spending a huge sum of money, then I shall retire uncomplainingly to some new and less notorious field of action.

"You will hear the cry at headquarters, and by the blood-suckers at the Imperial, as you heard it before when Stanfield ran against me, that nothing is being done, because they don't see my picture forty-seven times between a garage on Seventh Street and a second-hand dump on Stark."

McNary suggested that federal employees in Oregon should be required to contribute campaign money. To his brother, McNary wrote that U.S. Attorney Coke could help take responsibility for filling the campaign warchest. The elder McNary brother said that while such practices might be acceptable elsewhere in the country, the macing of federal workers would be frowned on in Oregon. "I cannot get over the absurdity of the proposition that these fellows holding federal jobs are to be immune in contributing to the campaign," the senator shot back. "They would not hold office thirty days after Baker took his seat here." Still grumbling, McNary contributed $1,000 to his re-election committee.

For the second time, McNary was campaigning from the Senate Office Building in Washington. That winter, he had introduced the most controversial legislation of his career, a farm-relief measure known as the McNary-Haugen bill. Senator Capper of Kansas, chairman of the farm bloc, endorsed McNary as "one of the strongest and most useful men in the Senate." Senator George Moses of New Hampshire, a flinty conservative, asserted that McNary had accomplished more than any other western senator. President Coolidge enhanced McNary's political stock with frequent invitations to the White House and a joint appearance with the Oregon Republican before newsreel cameras. McNary turned down his brother's suggestion that he solicit endorsements from Secretary of State Charles Evans Hughes and Secretary of Commerce Herbert Hoover, arguing that cabinet members should not interfere in primaries.

"Ninety-nine percent of the work must be done here by me, for I am running on my record," Charles wrote in mid-April. "It would be an entirely different proposition if I were running as an original candidate, then it would be necessary to use money for the purpose of self-exploitation. The fact is, if I had my way, I would not have any headquarters save the psychology it has upon a few friends. If I can beat Baker I can do it with or without the use of money."

McNary's campaign brochures highlighted his committee chairmanships and his "influence, power and prestige," claiming that he had delivered more than thirty-one million dollars in federal funds for Oregon. Mayor Baker charged that McNary was embellishing his record by taking credit for the efforts of the entire Oregon delegation. But this argument reinforced the fact that McNary had been highly effective in getting federal revenues.

The Klan's political machine had broken down. Intramural feuding had not only left the Klan divided in the Senate race but had led to charges of corruption against Gifford. A federal district court invalidated the compulsory school law on constitutional grounds that certified the Klan position as un-American. The Klan's two Multnomah County commissioners were indicted for alleged graft, and public revulsion against the Klan was growing. When Gifford attempted to switch his endorsement from Baker to McNary, it was spurned.

Winding up a 4,000-mile statewide campaign tour in which he made 114 speeches, Mayor Baker insisted that he was still confident of edging McNary. "The feeling out in the state—in eastern Oregon and southern Oregon and in the coast cities and counties has been an agreeable surprise," said Baker. "I have even greater confidence now than when I first started the campaign."

At the end of the primary campaign, McNary wrote privately: "The thing is over and god forbid that I shall ever go through another primary contest."

On 16 May 1924, McNary was renominated with an astonishing 64 percent of the vote sweeping every county in the state.

The senator's plurality over Baker was more than 55,000 votes. Most impressive of all, McNary carried Portland by a two-to-one ratio over its popular mayor. "I have been amazed at the vote I got," McNary told John. "How some of those far-off counties voted for me and in certain precincts throughout the state. It seemed to be spontaneous, because it came from every quarter."

Politically, the Klan was finished in Oregon. In future elections the secret society would try to help its favored candidates by spreading the word that they were backing someone else. McNary was furious that Gifford had purported to speak for him. "There were many ugly angles to the campaign," he told his brother, "and the worst of all the ginks, in my opinion, is this fellow Gifford. I never did trust that fellow, and as I look back over his whole connection with the campaign it has been as the trail of a serpent."

Elated by McNary's showing in the primary, Oregon Republican leaders promoted him as a vice-presidential contender at the 1924 GOP National Convention in Cleveland. The *Chicago Daily News* gave McNary favorable mention as a possible running-mate for President Coolidge, noting that the Oregon Republican would add strength to the ticket as a progressive, champion of agriculture, and westerner. When McNary said publicly that he was not interested in the office, the boomlet disappeared. Former Budget Director Charles Dawes wound up as Coolidge's vice presidential choice after Senator Borah and Illinois Governor Frank Lowden had both rejected the nomination.

McNary's first cousin, Milton A. Miller, was his Democratic opponent in the general election. White-haired and 64 years old, Miller was a former state legislator and mayor of Lebanon who had served as Oregon's Internal Revenue collector in the Wilson administration. "Cousin Milt" ran a gentlemanly campaign, taunting McNary for his Newberry vote and stressing progressive issues. Governor Walter Pierce and William Jennings Bryan both stumped for Miller. Pierce made an unsuccessful attempt to get Senator La Follette's endorsement for Miller. The Wisconsin senator, seeking the presidency as a Progressive third-party nominee, liked McNary. And, while in Oregon, La Follette's running-mate, Senator Burton K. Wheeler of Montana, came out for McNary's re-election.

In the November election, Senator McNary scored a clean sweep of Oregon's 36 counties, winning 66 percent of the vote and the highest vote ever received by an Oregon senatorial candidate. Now that the Klan's influence was broken, McNary soon made up for his earlier slight and named George Neuner as Oregon's U.S. Attorney.

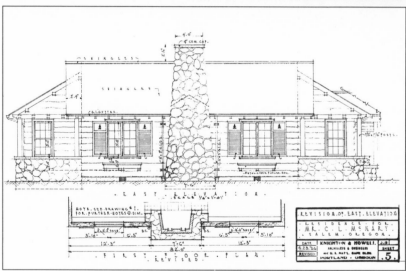

Fir Cone, McNary's Keizer farm, was part of his grandfather's pioneer homestead. Richard L. Neuberger described the farmhouse as Oregon's Monticello. (Author's collection)

In 1926, these plans (bottom) were drawn for the McNary's Fir Cone, outside Salem. (OHS collections)

9
Fir Cone

IN DECEMBER of 1923, McNary married Cornelia Morton in Chicago. They had met at a Washington dinner party and she later worked on his Senate staff. The strong-willed Cornelia soon grew bored with her secretarial job and left Capitol Hill to become Massachusetts director of the League of Women Voters. Following the death of his first wife, McNary gradually began dating and was widely regarded as one of Washington's most eligible men. And he remained in touch with Cornelia after she settled in Boston. Their marriage was splashed across Washington's society pages and not just because of McNary's growing political prominence. She was of the Maryland Calverts and a descendant of New York editor and onetime Democratic presidential nominee, Horace Greeley, who had advised his countrymen to "Go West."

While the Senate was in session, the McNarys lived in a succession of apartments at the Willard, Mayflower, and Hay-Adams hotels which, though fashionable and quite comfortable, were never a permanent home. Although McNary still owned the house on Court Street in Salem, his nephew Breyman Boise and his young family were now living there. After his remarriage, the Oregon senator began making plans for a summer home on a timbered pocket of his grandfather's homestead.

"I am coming home, and I want to have some place to go," McNary wrote his brother-in-law, W.T. Stolz, in the spring of 1926. "I don't want to have to impose upon my relatives or stay at the Marion Hotel or any other place in Salem. Hence the necessity of prompt action."

Sketching the architectural drawings for his farmhouse in 1925, McNary concentrated on a design that was simplicity itself. In a letter to Stolz, the senator said he had decided against one plan that "seemed to be a little artificial taken in connection with the larger aspects of the surroundings." The modest, white-frame house was constructed from McNary's blueprint at a cost of about $6,000.

McNary designed "Fir Cone" as an early nineteenth-century Cape Cod farmhouse and its simplicity preserved the woodland beauty of his estate. He would describe his home as "a typical ranch house." The center of the house was an enormous living room, 24 feet long and 18 feet wide, which had French doors and large picture windows. McNary's American history library was displayed in bookcases along the wall and a grand piano stood behind his favorite chair in a corner. In the middle of the room was a huge fireplace of native Willamette Valley stone. And hanging in the fire pit, held by Grandmother Claggett's pioneer crane, was a big iron kettle in which McNary cooked baked beans each day, adding generous portions of bacon, tomato sauce, brown sugar, and molasses. Flanking the living room on both sides were bedrooms and bathrooms. Service quarters were in the rear. McNary said that he had added only one spare room so that he would not be bothered by a houseful of guests. At each end of the house was a large stone porch where the senator often stretched out in his wicker chairs for relaxation.

Nothing refreshed McNary more than returning to Fir Cone and he never stopped thinking up new ideas for its 300 acres. "I have a really restful place here, picturesque and delightful—a regular old man's sanitorium," he wrote *Oregon Journal* Washington correspondent Carl Smith in the summer of 1927. "You do not hear anything about farm relief, politics, pests, and incompetents."

The setting was indeed spectacular with towering Douglas firs, 50 acres of lush green lawn, and two streams. Outside McNary's patio were geraniums, begonias, wisterias, honeysuckles, and hydrangeas and just beyond was a large flower garden with roses, dahlias, delphiniums and gigantic sweet peas. In a nearby grove was the senator's tennis court and a putting green.

McNary's trees were a lifelong passion. Collecting tree specimens from throughout North America and such distant lands as Spain and Lebanon, he developed an arboretum that became a national showcase. More than 250 acres of Fir Cone were covered with trees of all varieties, many of which had been cultivated by McNary himself. His principal crops were filberts, walnuts, cherries, and prunes, which were picked by the same farm workers for many years. McNary built a spiral staircase around a giant Douglas fir to a high lookout where he could survey the entire farm and, to the south, get a view of the sparkling bronze dome of the state capitol.

Tiny fir trees were carved into the green shutters of McNary's house and prickly cones were always dropping on the roof and lawn. McNary's personal letterhead simply said Fir Cone, Salem, Oregon. He liked the name of his farm so much that he officially registered it with the copyright office.

McNary prohibited hunting on his property, making it a bird and wildlife sanctuary whose population included scores of wild geese, ducks and pheasants. His favorites were the flock of Canadian honkers who remained at Fir Cone in defiance of migratory tradition. The senator fished in both streams and his favorite spot was a pond formed by LaBiche Creek. Before dropping his hook, McNary sprinkled liver across the water. "The fish are college educated," McNary observed. "As soon as you catch one, you won't catch any more." On McNary's pond, Senator James Couzens of Michigan caught his first Rainbow trout and at once became a fishing enthusiast.

Senator Couzens insisted that Fir Cone was the most restful and beautiful spot in America. Richard L. Neuberger, the gifted writer and historian who later held McNary's Senate seat, said that Fir Cone was "Oregon's Monticello" for a quarter of a century. And there were certain parallels between the farms in the green countrysides of Virginia and Oregon. Both McNary and Thomas Jefferson had been architects of their houses and viewed their farms as places of learned retreat. And both places would attract the nationally prominent and powerful as its guests, including presidents of the United States.

Formal entertaining was not the fashion at Fir Cone. McNary did not like large, dressy affairs. On Sundays, McNary's Salem relatives would join him for picnics on the vast, rolling lawn. Ella Stolz usually brought a potato salad and McNary ladled his rich baked beans. Cornelia sometimes gave afternoon teas for Salem and Portland friends.

McNary's favorite moments were walking among his trees with his dog Mickey. In 1927 the Oregon senator wrote this poem about his farm:

By the old Hallelujah fishpond, lookin' eastward from the sea,
There's a Mickey dog a setting and I know she thinks of me
For the wind is in the fir trees, and the sighing branches moan,
"Come Back, you Oregon solon, come you back to old Fir
    Cone."
Come you back to old Fir Cone,
To the comforts you have known,
Can't you 'ear the ducklin's quack from the creek there all
    alone?
On the road to old Fir Cone,
Where the speckled fishes drone,
An' the sun comes up a peepin' for my hidden, worn-out bone.

10

The Politics of Conservation

THROUGHOUT his Senate career, McNary's name was closely associated with the conservationist movement. An early follower of Gifford Pinchot, McNary was a staunch defender of the national forest system against its conservative critics. The Oregon senator joined forces with Pinchot and Secretary of Agriculture Henry C. Wallace in blocking Interior Secretary Albert Fall's proposed transfer of the Forest Service from the Department of Agriculture into the Interior Department. Fall was an outspoken advocate of the old-fashioned come-and-get-it style of lumbering and had attacked the Forest Service for "locking up" America's forest reserves from use. For a time, it appeared that Fall might gain President Harding's support for his scheme. But it collapsed when the Interior Secretary became entwined in the subterfuge of Teapot Dome, the Harding administration's most notorious giveaway scandal. Fall had used his government position to exploit public resources for his private enrichment. To restore confidence in the demoralized Interior Department, Harding sought McNary as his new Interior Secretary. However, McNary thought he could accomplish more by remaining in the Senate. His innovative leadership in conservation issues would soon confirm that he had made the right decision.

McNary became the intermediary between conservationists and the lumber industry in the bitter debate over federal regulation of forestry practices. Pinchot called for federal regulation of all private cutting and Senator Capper introduced legislation along those lines. Congressman Bertrand E. Snell of New York sponsored an alternative bill which provided federal aid to the states and granted autonomy to the states for setting their own forestry code. The lumber interests favored the Snell proposal. For months, both houses of Congress debated the rival bills and yet neither could muster a majority vote. Finally, McNary approached Colonel William B. Greeley, chief of the United States Forest Service, and told him that the Capper bill was "dead" and the Snell bill "bogged down."

"It's too big a dose for one bill," observed the Oregon senator. "What's the first thing to be done?"

"Stop the forest fires," Greeley responded.

"All right," said McNary, "we'll write a bill around that. But first we've got to build a fire under Congress. We must get more public interest behind the thing."

Within a short time, McNary drafted, and the Senate quickly adopted, a resolution directing the appointment of a Select Committee on Reforestation instructed "to investigate problems relating to reforestation, with a view to establishing a comprehensive national policy for lands chiefly suited for timber production in order to insure a perpetual supply of timber for the use and necessities of citizens of the United States."

On 3 January 1923, McNary was named chairman of this select committee whose members included senators Couzens of Michigan, Moses of New Hampshire, Harrison of Mississippi, and Fletcher of Florida. Beginning that winter, McNary presided over 24 hearings in 16 states, as well as those on Capitol Hill. At committee hearings in New Orleans, lumbermen of the old school claimed that it would be impractical to do anything but cut-out-and-get-out of logged-off land. The more enlightened Henry Hardtner told the committee about his young pine forests in northern Louisiana but said that it would require government help to prevent fires. When J. E. Rhodes of the Southern Pine Association urged federal regulations, McNary warned that such steps would be closer to "state dictatorship" than "government leadership." McNary supported federal-state cooperation in protecting the nation's forests, but without government regulation of timber cutting.

Along the way, Chief Forester Greeley took McNary and his colleagues on extensive side trips through logging camps and forests. "Chairman McNary accused me of trying to show them every tree in the United States," Greeley recalled years later. In Montana, the Oregon senator demanded to know why they were taking a back road to Spokane. The acerbic Senator Moses cracked, "The top sergeant says there are a million trees on this road, Charlie. We simply must see 'em."

Back in Washington, McNary wrote his brother on 28 March 1923: "I just returned today from a very interesting but strenuous trip through the southern states, studying many phases of reforestation. Our hearings were largely attended and I made addresses in a number of the southern cities. The South is certainly aroused over their disappearing forests."

Following the hearings, McNary issued the alarming report that less than 138 million acres of virgin timber remained standing of the original 800 million acres. There were, in addition, 81 million acres of logged-off land that could be reclaimed, McNary reported. Unless action were taken, McNary's report predicted future shortages of lumber. The timber supply, he said, "has already become too small to support the present consumption, and the depletion is steadily continuing."

"If there is any one thing that the whole country is interested in," McNary wrote John, "it is in the protection of our forests and I have an opportunity to do a grand piece of constructive work and I am going to do it. I shall introduce a bill and put it through the Senate and I think the Congress will know it as the McNary Reforestation Bill. It will provide the first great plan to conserve and protect forests."

In December 1923, McNary introduced his bill which provided for further acquisition of land for national forests, and federal-state cooperation with the lumber industry in reforestation. "The McNary bill," said Greeley, "freed forest purchases under the Weeks Law from the limitation to watersheds of navigable streams. It authorized the President to establish national forests on military and other federal reservations where the production of timber might be combined with other public uses and to add unreserved public lands to the national forests."

On 6 June 1924, McNary wired conservationist E.T. Allen: "SENATE JUST PASSED MY REFORESTATION BILL." Co-sponsored in the House of Representatives by New York Congressman John D. Clarke, it would become known as the Clarke-McNary act. President Coolidge signed the legislation the day after it passed the Senate. Secretary Wallace wrote McNary, "In my judgment, this measure is at least as important and significant as any previous action of Congress in developing a forest policy for the United States, and marks a very distinct forward step. We all greatly appreciate your good work."

In the next half century, 18 million acres would be reforested under terms of the Clarke-McNary Act. And in 1955, the U.S. Forest Service reported that 39 million acres were receiving forest-fire protection under its provisions. In that year alone, the federal government cooperated with the states in the planting of 50 million seedlings. McNary's legislation is still regarded as a major turning point in the history of American conservation. "Of all the men I have known in public life," Greeley wrote in his memoirs, "Senator McNary had the surest intuition of when to do something and just how to go about it."

One of McNary's Senate colleagues told Washington correspondents Joseph Alsop and Robert Kitner, "He'll rob the Treasury for forestry." Alsop and Kitner later wrote, "On the whole, Charles Linza McNary likes trees better than anything else in the world."

Senator McNary, working with Greeley and Earle Clapp, director of the Forest Service's bureau of research, introduced legislation that authorized a much more comprehensive forest research program. Ohio Congressman John R. McSweeney became McNary's co-sponsor in the House. And on 23 May 1928, the McNary-McSweeney Act was easily passed in both houses. Because of the Scottish ancestry of its chief sponsors, some foresters referred to it as "The Hoot-Mon Law." With a budget authorization of three million dollars, forestry's research bureau was greatly expanded. The activity at the Forest Products Laboratory in Madison, Wisconsin was stepped up as a result of McNary's legislation. In addition, McNary-McSweeney provided funding for a national network of Forest Experiment Stations. "The McNary-McSweeney Act also set in motion," Greeley said, "the gathering of vital statistics on national timber supply. It ordered an inventory of standing trees, their growth and the drain upon the resource from cutting, fire, and natural pests. In many parts of the country the survey gave us the first accurate measure of the growing power of our cutover forests."

McNary's forestry committee also investigated the problem of forest taxes and authorized an in-depth study by Yale University economist Fred R. Fairchild. "Heavy taxes have forced the owner of old-growth timber to cut his timber as rapidly as possible," stated the Forest Service's 1925 *Annual Report*. "This vicious race between forest destruction and mounting taxes has raised a fear that managed forests may be subjected to confiscatory taxation." As a direct result of Fairchild's study, Oregon and Washington passed tax incentives to encourage reforestation of logged-over areas.

The McNary-Woodruff Act of 1928 authorized eight million dollars for the expansion of national forests over the next three years and made it possible for even more acquisition of public land when states foreclosed on timber holdings for unpaid taxes and required federal management to prevent deterioration. When Senator L.S. Overman of South Carolina challenged the legislation on constitutional grounds, McNary countered that the government had the authority to acquire land for reforestation. The South Carolina Democrat withdrew his objection when McNary agreed to limit the federal government's purchase of land to one million acres in each state. In the spring of 1928, McNary-Woodruff swept through Congress and was signed into law by Coolidge.

As chairman of the Senate Committee on Irrigation and Reclamation from 1919 through 1926, McNary took an active role in supporting public development of the Tennessee, Colorado, and Columbia Rivers. He was closely aligned with Senator Norris in supporting federal development of Muscle Shoals and attacking proposed giveaways to private interests. President Coolidge vetoed Tennessee Valley legislation in 1928. McNary was successful in leading the fight for Boulder Dam on the Colorado River, which set the stage for his efforts in the Pacific Northwest during the New Deal. The Oregon senator considered his conservation and reclamation legislation as his most notable accomplishments. But his best known legislation was in a much different field and would launch a fundamental debate about the American future.

McNary and Haugen debate their farm measure with one of its leading critics, Secretary of Agriculture William Jardine, 1925. (Author's collection)

11

McNary-Haugen

McNARY was on the verge of national prominence, gaining increased recognition as a leader in the battle for farm relief. Entering the 1920s, American agriculture plunged into the worst farm depression in the nation's history. From the turn of the century until the Harding era, the American farmer had prospered as never before. During the World War, American farms had sustained the U.S. military effort and saved much of Europe from starvation. To keep up with popular demand in these boom years, a great many farmers bought expensive new farm machinery and took out second mortgages so they might acquire additional land. When the war ended, government price supports were eliminated and the foreign market all but disappeared as European farmers resumed normal food production. The average income per farm family dropped by nearly 50 percent in 1920. Thousands of farmers were left bankrupt and disillusioned, their farms and equipment sold at sheriffs' auctions. For the American farmer to be lifted out of the Depression, Oregon's senior senator concluded that bold and unprecedented measures were necessary.

As it turned out, an Illinois manufacturer of farm machinery, George N. Peek, had come up with just such a plan, which he called "equality for agriculture. "Peek called for federal aid in removing price-depressing surpluses from the domestic market and selling them abroad at the world price. His plan attempted to apply the protective principle of the tariff to "do for agriculture what it does for industry." Any losses to the federal treasury would be covered by an assessment or tax on each commodity sold by the farmer. The special tax was termed an "equalization fee." Secretary of Agriculture Henry C. Wallace was very much impressed with Peek's idea and sought to have it introduced in Congress. In December of 1923, Secretary Wallace and George C. Jewett, manager of the American Wheat Growers Associated, sold McNary on preparing Peek's draft into workable legislative form.

On 16 January 1924, Senator McNary and Iowa Congressman Gilbert N. Haugen, chairman of the House Agriculture Committee, formally introduced the McNary-Haugen bill. Their legislation would spark the chief ideological debate of the Twenties. Although offered as an emergency farm-relief measure, McNary-Haugan called for nothing less than a fundamental change in the role of American government. It challenged the old truths of social Darwinism and laissez-faire economics, for its premise was that government had a responsibility to promote economic and social justice in hard times. Like the Populist movement of the 1890s, McNary-Haugenism became a struggle between the farm belt and industrial America. And like its forerunner, McNary-Haugenism was denounced by conservatives as radical and economically unsound. Both its supporters and critics sensed that McNary-Haugen raised important questions about the direction of American life.

"I shall in a few days from now propose the wheat bill, which I know will give me a tremendous amount of publicity among the rural population," McNary wrote his brother on 11 January. The bill called for the establishment of a federal farm board which would purchase surplus agricultural commodities and sell them abroad. The bill also provided for a two-price ratio, with a high domestic price and a lower export price that would be set by the government."

McNary-Haugen got more attention in the public prints than any other farm legislation in memory. "I think my wheat bill was a ten strike," McNary wrote John on 25 January. "I am getting telegrams from all over the state supporting the so-called McNary-Haugen wheat bill. It is a terribly complicated measure and I have given it a world of study, but I don't know whether it will get through Congress or not."

Nor did other political observers. "Great pressure is being brought upon the President to endorse my wheat bill," McNary reported home on 14 February. "I don't know what he will do. Supporters of the bill are here on the ground and a great many of them are overflowing my offices today and are holding a consultation there now."

To his friend Louis Lachmund, McNary wrote, "I am terribly busy with my wheat bill. That has given me ten times the work my reforestation bill and report did and I am receiving letters and petitions and telegrams from all over the country." On 9 March, he told his brother, "I have never gotten into quite as complicated a piece of legislation in my life, with ramifications in all directions in the field of economics and it is complex and inexplicable."

Unprepared for the McNary-Haugen groundswell, the Coolidge Administration joined forces with big business in opposing farm relief. The U.S. Chamber of Commerce actively worked against McNary-Haugen. So did numerous economists, conservative Democratic leaders, and eastern publishers. Kansas Agricultural College president, William M. Jardine, denounced it as "a very unsound, unsafe measure" which placed the government "into the most gigantic business known in history." The *Wall Street Journal* asserted that if McNary-Haugen would be enacted, the "American people will pay dearly for an unwise experiment in socialism and government price-fixing."

McNary-Haugen supporters argued that the legislation would stimulate the nation's economy. The American Farm Bureau Federation said the farm-relief plan would bring a billion dollars to the farmers and "everybody will share in their increased prosperity." Bernard Baruch, the politically ambitious Wall Street financier who had served as chairman of the War Industries Board, became one of the bill's most visible and energetic backers. "Equality for agriculture is what the farmer is striving for," declared Baruch. "Other industries are organized and farming is not. It should be unnecessary for the farmer to sell competatively and the fixing of the price of his total production by the surplus that comes in competition with the cheapest labor in the world should be prevented. The provisions of the McNary bill will do that."

On 3 June 1924, the industrial north and cotton south combined to defeat McNary-Haugen in the House of Representatives by a vote of 223 to 155. While the bill's rejection came as a disappointment to its chief sponsor, McNary and his allies gave notice that their battle for farm parity had only begun.

As a result of McNary-Haugen, the Oregonian was receiving more mail from rural areas than any other senator and nearly all of the letters urged him to keep up the good fight. In the hot summer weeks of 1924, Peek, Jewett, and the agriculture secretary's son, Henry A. Wallace, editor of *Wallace's Farmer*, organized a coalition that would make McNary-Haugen a national crusade. Their group was called the American Council of Agriculture. And Peek started working full-time in pushing McNary-Haugen before a national audience.

McNary-Haugen surfaced as a major issue in the 1924 presidential campaign. In the Republican primaries, Senator Hiram Johnson of California embraced McNary-Haugenism and upset Coolidge in South Dakota. But Silent Cal easily won renomination at the Cleveland convention, which ignored McNary-Haugen in its platform, though called for more adequate tariff protection for the farmer. The Democratic and Progressive party platforms both endorsed the McNary farm-relief plan. Even so, McNary would not bolt the GOP and joined the overwhelming majority of the agricultural population who supported Coolidge's re-election. Although the president distrusted anything that could be called progressive, the Oregon senator held out hope that Coolidge would agree to at least some federal aid for the farmer. On 4 November Coolidge retained the presidency in a Republican landslide.

A few days before the election, McNary's cause was dealt a major blow when Secretary Wallace died. The agriculture secretary had been McNary's staunchest ally in the Harding and Coolidge administrations and the godfather of McNary-Haugenism. Only recently Wallace had completed a book in support of McNary-Haugen. Coolidge offered Wallace's department to Herbert Hoover, but the Commerce secretary wanted to remain where he was. Within the administration, Hoover had been the most outspoken opponent of McNary-Haugen, attacking it as socialism. Coolidge's proposed move of Hoover to the Agriculture Department gave a strong signal that he would not accept McNary's legislation in any form. The president told Senator Capper, leader of the farm bloc, that 79 names were under consideration for the job. Asked if he were interested, the Kansas Republican replied that he preferred staying in the Senate. Hoover and Capper both recommended the appointment of Kansas educator William J. Jardine whose vocal opposition to McNary-Haugen made him more than acceptable to Coolidge. When Jardine took office, McNary knew that it lengthened the odds against his measure.

Undeterred, the Oregon Republican introduced his farm-relief bill for a second time on 3 February 1925. Within four weeks, it was reported favorably by the Senate Agriculture Committee, but it was too late in the winter session for anything more. On the final day of the session, Senator R. B. Howell of Nebraska tacked it on as an amendment to the Omnibus Naval Bill. The Republican-controlled Senate turned down Howell's amendment by a vote of 69 to 17.

Throughout 1925, McNary-Haugenism was gathering momentum at a fast pace. Behind the scenes, the Oregon senator picked up the support of bluff, sharp-spoken Vice President Charles G. Dawes. Still later in the year came the politically valuable endorsement of former Illinois Governor Frank Lowden, who had previously called for single-commodity marketing cooperatives run by farmers. To many businessmen and political leaders, Lowden's conversion to McNary-Haugenism gave the radical legislation a strong credibility boost. So, too, did the qualified endorsement of the well-regarded British economist, Sir Josiah Stamp.

In an effort to expand the McNary-Haugen legislative coalition, Peek broadened the measure to include cotton with such basic commodities as wheat, corn, butter, cattle, and hogs. The Oregon senator gave his approval in the hope of attracting southern support with the addition of cotton.

On 7 December 1925, President Coolidge went before the American Farm Bureau Federation's national convention and made a scathing attack on McNary-Haugenism. The delegates gave Coolidge a frosty reception and passed a resolution demanding quick enactment of a farm relief plan that was unmistakably McNary's.

The Senate debated McNary's revised bill in early June of 1926. "I am having a struggle with farm relief," McNary wrote W. T. Stolz on 3 June. "Spoke two and a half hours yesterday and will speak and hour and a half again today. That is a hard proposition and I shall be glad when the session is over, particularly when this subject is out of the Senate."

Testifying in opposition, Secretary of the Treasury Andrew Mellon asserted that McNary-Haugen's adoption would be a disaster for American industry. For less selfish reasons, Hoover worked against the measure, contending that it was government price-fixing.

"I expect a vote on my bill today," McNary wrote his brother on 24 June. "I will be tickled to death when it is over, whatever the results may be. I have had four weeks pull and haul and strain that has been hard to endure."

On that same day, McNary-Haugen II was voted down by a count of 45 to 39. "There is a gentleman, named Mr. Farm Relief, who I don't want to look in the face for a long while," the Oregon senator wrote privately. "He has pretty nearly made me look like Firpo, after he stayed two rounds with Dempsey." McNary's reference was to an Argentine heavyweight who had recently lost a bloody fight with world heavyweight champion Jack Dempsey.

Shortly after this setback, McNary had some good news. His old friend Senator Norris told him that he was stepping down as chairman of the Agriculture Committee, which meant the Oregon Republican would take over his favorite committee. In his memoirs, Norris wrote that his duties "had become too heavy and should go to a younger man." Noting that McNary was next in line, the Nebraska liberal said, "We had worked together and I had the highest regard for him and for his outlook on national affairs. I wanted him to have the chairmanship, and my resignation paved the way for his advancement."

McNary had achieved his longtime goal. "I am now in complete command of the whole agricultural proposition," he wrote his brother. "I will have more room, and a large, spacious, convenient, committee room. I will enjoy the work because it is in my line."

Back in Oregon, the senator was vague about the future of McNary-Haugen. "What action will be taken at the next session of Congress is beyond prediction. The economic conditions of the farmers in the various farming sections will probably be the determining factor."

Before long, the farm situation had worsened. Cotton prices dropped by half and were still falling because of an enormous surplus. Enactment of McNary-Haugen would have prevented this crisis, cotton farmers argued. In November of 1926, a national farm-relief conference was called in St. Louis. The farmers attending this gathering demanded the swift approval of McNary-Haugen, warning legislators that those who voted against it would do so at their own peril.

A month later, McNary introduced a third version of his farm bill, which would establish a federal farm board to handle surplus crops through cooperatives. Under the revised McNary-Haugen bill, the equalization fee was to be collected from the middle men instead of the producers. Until the tax had been collected, a $250 million appropriation would cover the farm board's expenses. "The bill is essentially a surplus-control bill," said McNary, "the sole aim being to stabilize prices through control of the surplus."

At times, McNary seemed to be running short on patience. "Really I am getting so fed up on farm measures, farm relief, farm problems and farm grief that I want for rest and quiet," he wrote W. T. Stolz in January. On 8 February, McNary told his brother, "I will surely be glad when the final vote is taken on my farm relief measure. We had a night session last night, running until eleven o'clock. Early morning committees and listening to the farm propagandists and maneuvering for position and discussing the amendments and substitutes keeps me in more or less of a whirl."

On 11 February 1927, McNary's farm bill passed the Senate by a 47 to 39 margin. Six days later, McNary-Haugen was approved by the House of Representatives with Southern congressmen providing the winning votes. The Oregon senator received acclaim as a master strategist. "No name has impressed itself more indelibly upon the politics of the current era than that of Charles L. McNary," said one national magazine. "Mr. McNary is the champion of the issue destined to remain paramount until it emerges from the field of controversy into the statute books."

President Coolidge was unmoved. He rejected a conciliatory veto message that had been written by Milton S. Eisenhower, a young official in the Agriculture Department, and issued a sharply worded veto. McNary-Haugen, said Coolidge, went against "an economic law as well established as any law of nature." The president claimed that it would mean government price-fixing and "the most vicious form of taxation." Moreover, Coolidge said the whole idea was unconstitutional. Lacking the votes to override the veto, McNary sought an alternative farm-relief measure that would meet White House approval.

Despite their ideological differences, the Oregon senator and Coolidge were on cordial terms. "I always liked the little fellow and I believe the feeling was mutual," McNary would later write. The Oregon Republican spent several weekends with the Coolidges on the *Mayflower*, the presidential yacht, and the McNarys were frequently invited to White House dinners and receptions. Coolidge consulted with him on a regular basis and treated him more generously on patronage than earlier presidents had. John McNary was named by Coolidge to the federal district court, which established the McNary clan as Oregon's reigning political dynasty.

When Coolidge nominated another Oregonian, Judge Wallace McCamant, for the Circuit Court of Appeals, McNary led the fight for Senate confirmation. Six years earlier, McCamant had stood on a chair and lifted Coolidge from obscurity by nominating him for the vice presidency. Without the Oregon judge's impulsive gesture, it is doubtful that Coolidge would have ever reached the White House. McNary tried to help Coolidge repay this political debt. The nomination was immediately challenged by California's Senator Johnson, who had a grudge to settle. At the 1920 convention, the Oregon delegation was committed to Johnson, winner of the Oregon primary. Most Oregon GOP leaders, including McNary, had supported Johnson. But Judge McCamant refused to vote for Johnson in Chicago. The California senator declared that the judge's defiance of Oregon law meant that he was unfit for the federal bench. Appearing before the Senate Judiciary Committee, Judge McCamant defended his 1920 convention vote on grounds that Johnson had betrayed the GOP in running for the vice presidency on the Progressive ticket in 1912. The judge then questioned the patriotism of Johnson and Teddy Roosevelt, a serious mistake.

McNary was appalled by Judge McCamant's graceless performance and concluded that his attack on Roosevelt and Johnson had doomed his nomination. The Oregon senator advised Coolidge to withdraw McCamant's name or face almost certain defeat on the Senate floor. The President left it to the judge and McCamant refused to quit without a fight. His nomination was sent to the Senate floor with a negative recommendation from the Judiciary Committee. Then without debate or a roll call, the Senate rejected McCamant's nomination. Describing the whole episode as "unpleasant," McNary seemed relieved when it was over.

In the spring of 1927, Coolidge and McNary often conferred over breakfasts of scrambled eggs, sausage, and buckwheat pancakes with maple syrup from the president's native Vermont. Their discussions focused on farm-relief and McNary indicated his willingness to eliminate most of the features objectionable to the administration. Encouraged by these talks, McNary began drafting a compromise farm-relief plan.

McNary's name was frequently mentioned in the public print as a vice-presidential contender for 1928. The president had soured on Dawes and the conventional wisdom was that he would select another running-mate. To many political observers, Coolidge and McNary appeared to be the strongest possible combination. C. Bascom Slemp, Coolidge's executive assistant and Virginia GOP national committeeman, told the Oregon senator that he would be the ideal choice and reported that McNary was especially popular in the South. Senator George H. Moses of New Hampshire endorsed McNary for the vice presidency. The *Washington Star* said that McNary's selection would balance the ticket geographically and philosophically. "What would be more natural to put some favorite of the Western farmers on the ticket with him?" asked the *Philadelphia Public Ledger*. "Coolidge and McNary would make a nice Eastern and Western ticket."

"The President needs a farm bill, and he desperately needs Mr. McNary's name on it," Frank Kent reported in *Collier's*. "And Mr. McNary desires with all his heart to be second name on the ticket of Coolidge and McNary in 1928. You can't persuade Mr. McNary that any other Republican would make so glorious a run next time as Mr. Coolidge. Any other candidate would be likely to come from too near Oregon. . . . For the President, Mr. McNary's name on a Coolidge farm bill will be a sort of blown-in-the-bottle evidence that the bill will cure all the ills that the farmers ever have, ever will have or can suffer from."

McNary never mentioned the vice presidency in his frequent letters to relatives. Having just moved into the chairmanship of the Senate Agriculture Committee, it seems unlikely that he would have wanted to step down for a job which he perceived as largely ceremonial. The Oregon senator also knew that, unlike other political offices, the vice-presidency was that rare situation where the office sought the man. Nobody could campaign for vice president. The choice was the presidential candidate's alone. Whether McNary had national ambitions or not, he was fully aware that the exposure in magazines and leading newspapers was politically helpful and he did nothing to discourage such speculation.

On 2 August 1927, Coolidge ended all talk of a dream ticket with McNary, announcing that he did "not choose to run for President in 1928." When Coolidge issued his laconic statement, McNary was in Seattle and expressed his belief that the president was still available for another term. "It's a tribute to the President's modesty and a mark of proper prudence on his part. It also serves notice on the people that he will not be mixed up in any knockdown and drag-out fight. In fact, I think he will be nominated and re-elected."

Back in Washington, *Oregon Journal* correspondent Carl Smith wrote McNary: "Whether Calvin meant it or not, I believe he is fairly out of it. The country has accepted the statement at face value, and the active candidates will occupy the field without much elbow room remaining."

With Coolidge a lame duck, the spotlight suddenly shifted to Herbert Hoover, Frank Lowden, and other Republican hopefuls for 1928. The Oregon senator continued seeking Coolidge's support for farm-relief legislation. In the *Country Gentleman*, McNary wrote, "I am not indissolubly wedded and joined to any relief proposition thus far put forward. Neither the idea of a farm board nor any particular method of appointing it, nor any feature of the farm-relief act passed by the 69th Congress is so sacred to me that I would try to prevent modification or elimination if a better plan comes to light."

In late October, McNary returned to the nation's capital with a pledge that the fight would go on. "What form legislation takes is not so important," he said, "so long as our guide is the principle that agriculture must be restored to its former place of equality with industry, transportation, and labor." In December, the Oregon senator berated Coolidge for not showing movement on farm-relief in his message to Congress.

Early in 1928, McNary put together a fourth version of McNary-Haugen that included some major concessions designed to gain the administration's backing. The 1928 measure was extended to all crops, and the makeup of the federal farm board would be determined by the president. McNary had considered dropping the equalization fee but backed off when farm leaders objected.

On 12 April McNary gave a strong defense of the equalization fee when Senator F. M. Sackett of Kentucky made a motion
that it be eliminated. "This is the heart of the proposal," replied
McNary, "and the first time in four years we have met the issue
fairly. The surplus has created out problem. The farmer needs
the equalization fee. He wants no present benefit without pay-
ing for it. He has always fought subsidies of every kind. They
do not want taxpayer's money. They want an opportunity to be
placed on an equal footing with industry and labor—they are
willing to pay the cost themselves.

"You can take the measure and emasculate it and make it look
attractive to the unthinking individual or the individual who
has not at heart the interest of the farmer permanently and
vote this equalization fee out. If you do, my friends, I warn you,
you will not be back here another year asking for an appropriation. That will be the finish of legislation for the farmer."

In a roll call vote, the Sackett amendment was defeated by a
vote of 46 to 31. On the same day, McNary-Haugen IV prevailed in the Senate by a 53 to 23 count. On 3 May, it passed in
the House by a vote of 204 to 121. "Thank heaven, the old relief
bill is over and I do feel the need of a little relief," McNary
wrote his sister. "It was a terrible strain and quite a victory. I
received many glad words at the conduct of the farm-relief bill
and my speech in its behalf."

For all the excitement, McNary still needed Coolidge's signature. On 21 May, the president called McNary to the Oval
Office and told him of his intention to veto the Oregon senator's
farm bill. McNary found Coolidge uninformed and uncaring
about the farm depression. To his brother, he observed that what
Coolidge "doesn't know about 'sech' things would fill a great
big library." In his veto message, Coolidge attacked McNary-
Haugen as "a system of wholesale commercial doles" and "bureaucracy gone mad."

Coolidge's veto, said McNary, showed "that the President is
unsympathetic with the farmer and unfamiliar with his problems." On 23 May, he told Nina, "Today the President took a
club to my farm bill and sent to Congress a very peppy veto in-
dicating want of knowledge of the subject matter. However, he
has to rely on others and they are not friendly to any farm
measures."

Two days later, McNary asked his colleagues to override the
president's veto. "In my judgment," he declared, "the message

of the President sets forth no new reasons, it makes no new arguments not heretofore made. Indeed, it is bottomed on misunderstandings which have always been the weapon of those who oppose legislation of this character." Although McNary's forces came close, they were four votes short of the two-thirds vote required to block Coolidge's veto.

Henry A. Wallace called the president's strident veto message "a slap in the face for agriculture." Columbia University economist Rexford G. Tugwell said it demonstrated Coolidge's "stubborn determination to do nothing." It shook the faith of a great many farmers in the GOP. Nearly a generation later, Alf M. Landon said that a key factor in President Truman's upset victory over Thomas E. Dewey had been the "deep-seated distrust of the Republican party by farmers ever since President Calvin Coolidge vetoed the McNary-Haugen bills in the '20s."

During a troubled era, Senator McNary had brought hope to the American farmer. And, for the remainder of his political career, McNary would be a political hero in the farm belt. Although the legislation had its flaws, it had been a bold attempt to redefine the role of American government. Samuel Eliot Morison has written that Coolidge's vetoes left American farmers "far more vulnerable than they need have been to the Great Depression." McNary's legislation was the forerunner of the anti-depression measures of Franklin D. Roosevelt's New Deal.

McNary and Iowa Congressman Gilbert N. Haugen were the co-sponsors of farm-relief legislation that would spark the major political debate of the 1920s. (Author's collection)

McNary at Nevada's Boulder Dam, ca. 1930. This great irrigation and flood-control ediface would eventually be renamed
Hoover Dam, after McNary's old boyhood friend and fierce political opponent, President Herbert Hoover. (Author's collection)

12

McNary and Hoover

FROM THE BEGINNING of the 1928 presidential campaign, Herbert Hoover was the betting favorite. Even before Coolidge's surprise announcement, Hoover was the most towering figure in the administration. "Secretary of Commerce Hoover had had me over several times and again a few mornings ago, telling me about his plans," McNary wrote his brother on 21 March 1928. "He thinks he can win, and I rather think he can, though I think he is beatable if the opposition could employ skillful hands."

McNary had known Hoover longer than anyone in Washington. They had been friends since boyhood when both lived in Salem. Although they were the same age, different interests kept the youngsters from genuine intimacy. McNary said later that his decision to attend Stanford had been influenced by Hoover's earlier example. While McNary returned to their hometown, Hoover embarked for distant parts of the world as a mining engineer. By the time Hoover was 40, he was a multimillionaire. Both McNary and Hoover came to Washington in 1917 and resumed their friendship. As the food administrator, Hoover became one of the stars of the Wilson cabinet. In 1918, Hoover provided McNary with a well-timed endorsement in his tough primary fight. Following the Armistice, they were allies in supporting U.S. entry into the League of Nations. In 1920, Hoover was seriously mentioned for both the Democratic and Republican presidential nominations, winning the Michigan primary as a Democrat. Franklin D. Roosevelt was among Hoover's early supporters. But in March, Hoover killed his chances by declaring himself an independent progressive and attacking both parties.

In McNary's judgment, Hoover was politically naive. "A bonehead play," the Oregon senator said of Hoover's 1920 announcement. "He would have been in a much stronger position had he kept silent six weeks longer."

While Hoover failed to win either nomination, he rebounded after the election to become secretary of commerce in the Harding cabinet. For the next eight years, he was the most creative and visible member of the cabinet. With notable success, he promoted foreign trade and fought international cartels in raw materials. He also pushed arms control, conservation, and such social reforms as the abolition of child labor. When more than one million people were left homeless in the Mississippi flood of 1927, Hoover personally directed the massive relief effort. For all his good work, Hoover thought there were definite limits to the role government should play in the nation's economy. So, despite the farm depression of the Twenties, Hoover strongly opposed the McNary-Haugen plan because it conflicted with his ideology of American individualism.

Heading into the campaign, McNary-Haugen loomed as the dominant issue. Because Hoover was the only Republican contender who opposed it, he was the only candidate acceptable to Coolidge. The president's men, led by political strategist C. Bascom Slemp, were actively working for Hoover. Meanwhile, leaders of the farm bloc suggested that McNary seek the presidency. A national farm magazine poll indicated considerable strength for a McNary candidacy.

Senator Arthur Capper of Kansas, chairman of the farm bloc and publisher of the nation's largest chain of farm journals, wrote McNary: "Now, Charles, it is going to be up to you to save the country at the next session of Congress and hold the Republican Party intact in this section of the country when the campaign starts. You can count on any help I can give; furthermore if you will run for president or vice-president, I am for you."

McNary was enough of a realist, however, to know that his chances of winning the nomination would be remote at a convention run by the party's Old Guard. With the Oregon senator out of the running, there was no shortage of Republicans seeking to become the farmer's standard-bearer. Former Illinois

Governor Frank Lowden, and senators George Norris of Nebraska, Charles Curtis of Kansas, and James Watson of Indiana all plunged into the race. Actively courted by the GOP hopefuls, McNary remained neutral. "I really don't care who is president," he explained to his brother. "That sounds strange to the folks at home or those out of the political life at Washington. I like all of their runners-up, and in the end would get just as many trips on the Mayflower with one as with the other, just as many hot cakes and eggs at the White House breakfasts, and about as much recognition and federal patronage, though in the latter field they are not worth much."

Running against such a large field worked to Hoover's advantage. Though Norris clobbered him in Wisconsin, Hoover won impressively in California, Ohio, Michigan, Massachusetts, New Jersey, Maryland, and Oregon. Well before the convention, Hoover appeared to have locked up the nomination.

When the Republican Convention opened at Kansas City on 12 June, hundreds of farmers demonstrated against Hoover outside of Civic Auditorium. Hoover's nomination, warned farm leaders, would touch off a farm rebellion against the GOP. During the convention, McNary conferred with Hoover in Washington on relief for the farmers. Quietly and purposefully, the two Republican leaders attempted to work out their differences. McNary agreed to yield on the controversial equalization fee and Hoover committed himself to acknowledging the federal government had responsibility for the economic welfare of the nation's farmers, telling McNary that he would support a federal farm board with the funding and authority to deal with the farm surplus and stabilize farm prices. Hoover was easily nominated on the first ballot and chose a McNary-Haugen supporter, Senate Majority Leader Charles Curtis, as his vice-presidential candidate. Farm spokesmen said they were not appeased by the selection of Curtis and renewed their threat to defect from the party.

On the day after the convention, McNary held another meeting with Hoover and reached final agreement on their compromise farm-relief plan. Hoover had given the Oregon senator a commitment to farmers which Harding and Coolidge had refused to make. And McNary, for his part, pledged to help head off an anti-Hoover farm revolt. As he strode out of the Commerce Department, McNary described Hoover as "sympathetic and anxious to relieve the distress of the farm population."

McNary told reporters that he would throw all his political strength in support of Hoover and Curtis.

McNary's endorsement provided Hoover with a major boost. "Secretary Hoover's first victory in his election campaign," reported the *New York Herald Tribune*, "was the coming of Senator McNary of Oregon to pledge his support." Added the *Philadelphia Inquirer*, "It is likely to become the most important victory of the entire campaign." The *Raleigh News and Observer*, denouncing McNary's compact with Hoover, editorialized, "Senator McNary has forfeited the confidence of all farmers." Congressman Haugen of Iowa, McNary's co-sponsor, disavowed the Hoover-McNary agreement, saying that the Oregon senator should not have given up the equalization fee. But, in the end, Haugen and most of the congressional farm bloc joined McNary in supporting Hoover.

Later in the summer, the Democratic convention nominated New York Governor Alfred E. Smith for president and included the principles of McNary-Haugen in the party platform. When Smith came out in favor of the farm relief measure, he gained the support of McNary allies George Norris, farm editor Henry A. Wallace, and George Peek, the originator of the McNary-Haugen plan.

McNary was one of Hoover's most active campaigners that fall, spending most of his time in the farm belt states. His Chicago speech was broadcast over a national radio hookup. "Mr. Hoover has greater knowledge of the economics of farm distribution than any man in the United States," he declared. "I believe under his leadership the farm problem will be effectively and permanently solved."

The Oregon senator had never cared much for the campaign trail and his efforts for Hoover left him exhausted. "I certainly did my bit and it was a hard proposition," he wrote his brother. "I spent eight straight nights in the sleeper and was badly bunged up." But, at the end of his tour, McNary concluded, "I'm glad I made the circuit for the party, met lots of people who were all nice to me and had good crowds, and they told me I got by in good shape. Nearly every state put in its claim, not for personal reasons but for notoriety of the bill bearing in part my name."

In his travels, McNary sensed that the religious issues would play a larger role in the outcome of the election than had been acknowledged in the public print. Because Smith was a Catholic, McNary found evidence of major Democratic defections in Protestant border states. "I think we each agree that Mr. Hoover will receive the election," he wrote John, "because of issues much deeper than some being politely discussed."

On 6 November 1928, Hoover won big. McNary's prediction about the religious issue turned out to be accurate. Smith lost seven states in the previously solid, Democratic South. Hoover also carried every state where McNary had campaigned. "Wonderful," the Oregon Senator wired Hoover, "We will now solve the vexing farm problem."

Within a few days, Hoover established his headquarters for the transition period on the same floor as McNary's apartment as the Mayflower Hotel. Soon afterward, Hoover offered to name the Oregon senator as secretary of agriculture or secretary of the interior. Though flattered, McNary told Hoover that he could be more useful in the Senate. The president-elect later chose Arthur Hyde, a Missouri car dealer, as agriculture secretary, and Stanford University President Ray Lyman Wilbur as interior secretary.

On a rainy March afternoon, McNary watched Hoover take the presidential oath on the east front of the Capitol. McNary got drenched and caught a bad cold. "The day was one of the worst of the year," McNary wrote his sister. "It's history that all inaugural days have been inconspicuous by their indecency."

McNary wasted no time in scheduling hearings on the Hoover administration's farm bill, the Agricultural Marketing Act. The measure was similar to the McNary-Haugen bill but without the equalization fee. In the committee room, McNary scolded his old friend L.J. Taber of the National Grange for trying to amend the legislation to include an export debenture. Hoover had made it known that he would veto the farm bill unless it met his specifications. On 15 June 1929, the Senate passed a clean bill. When Hoover signed it into law, he presented McNary with the pen at an Oval Office ceremony.

On 15 July 1929, the Federal Farm Board went into business. With a budget of $151 million, the FFB was supposed to stabilize farm prices by providing farmers with assistance in marketing and storing their produce, developing new byproducts, and controlling production. But it never had a chance. Just three months later, the stock market collapsed in the worst crash in American history. The Great Depression had begun and nobody was hit harder than the farmers. The prices of wheat, cotton, and corn collapsed and thousands of farmers went broke along with the banks that held their loans. In three years, the FFB lost more that $345 million buying surplus farm products, and yet prices continued to fall. McNary submitted a new farm relief plan with the equalization fee aimed at raising prices. But Hoover, disappointed at the FFB's failure, still rejected McNary-Haugensim. McNary thought that Hoover's response to the Depression had been adequate. The President got pledges from industry to maintain current employment and wage levels, and labor leaders promised not to strike. Hoover urged state and local governments to increase their funding for public works in order to create more jobs. He also increased federal spending for public works and called on private organizations to help provide emergency relief to the poor. It soon became apparent that Hoover's efforts were not enough. As conditions got worse, Hoover lost credibility by suggesting that things were not as bad as they seemed. Yet by the winter of 1931–32, *Fortune* magazine reported that 10 million Americans, one-fourth of the nation's work force, were jobless. The Hoover administration claimed that the number was 2.5 million.

Despite his reputation as a great humanitarian, Hoover refused to have any personal contact with the victims of the Depression. When an aide, not knowing of Hoover's attitude, had him driven past a breadline of people in threadbare clothing, the president would not look at them and ordered his aide never to bring him anywhere near those people again. It was not that he did not care. Hoover was deeply troubled by the anguish and suffering. But his aloofness made him appear to be insensitive to their plight. Within a short time, Hoover had become the scapegoat for the Depression. The shantytowns in which thousands of jobless families lived were called "Hoovervilles." Cars driven by mules, because their owners could not afford gasoline were nicknamed "Hoovercarts." There were no old-age pensions and no unemployment benefits. Millions of Americans were utterly destitute. Some families dug for rotten food in city dumps, while others waited outside the back doors of restaurants for table scraps. Hoover suggested that what the nation needed was a "big laugh" to make people forget their troubles.

McNary thought emergency relief would be a more appropriate response to the Depression. But Hoover flatly opposed the dole, saying his goal was to "preserve the principles of individual and local responsibility." McNary agreed with Hoover's conservative principles, yet he was quicker to recognize that old-fashioned ideals were not going to end the crisis. The Oregon senator was more interested in getting results than upholding the past. "We have plenty of precedents in relief extended so generously to foreign nations and to people in various states who have suffered from droughts and unreasonable conditions," McNary declared in calling for more money for the Depression's victims. Hoover said in later years that McNary was "a shade too radical."

Even when they were on the same side politically, McNary and Hoover were uneasy in their alliance. Indeed, McNary found him so somber that he would get out of meeting with him when it was possible to do so without embarrassment. McNary declined an invitation to spend the weekend with the Hoovers at the president's retreat in the Blue Ridge mountains, explaining that he had "an important conference," which, in truth, was his regular Saturday golf with colleagues. "I did not want to go at all because it is an awful bore once you have had the experience," McNary wrote his sister Nina. "I enjoy being with Hoover a little but I don't get awfully exhilarated, and I would a lot rather be with my friends at Burning Tree." In a letter to his brother, McNary added, "Last Saturday I got out of going with the President on a fishing trip to the Rapidan because really it is not very interesting on those trips with the President because most of the time is spent playing ping-pong, pitching horseshoes, or looking in the fireplace."

Several weeks later, Hoover invited McNary again and this time he accepted. The president's limousine took the senator and Cornelia through the mountains to the Hoover cabin on the Headwaters of the Rapidan. Hoover, McNary, and journalist Mark Sullivan went fishing, hiked up the mountainside, and talked politics. "We had a lovely dinner in the camp in the evening and the President and I discussed his treaty message and legislation and lots of things," McNary wrote Nina. According to McNary, Hoover "was very cordial and most appreciative of what he called my splendid work in handling the situation in the Senate."

By the middle of his term, Hoover had soured on McNary. Always sensitive, the Republican president resented the Oregon senator's low-key yet biting criticism of his administration. McNary regarded Hoover as a well-intentioned businessman who simply was not up to the demands of the presidency. What bothered McNary the most about Hoover was his political ineptitude. "If the engineer who was successful in Africa had more political acumen," he wrote John, "mole hills would not be viewed as mountains and tempests would take place at sea rather than in the teapot."

In the spring of 1930, McNary played a leading role in the rejection of Hoover's nominee for the Supreme Court, Judge John J. Parker of North Carolina. While the senator felt that presidents were entitled to make their own appointments, McNary was less inhibited in opposing lifetime judicial appointments and several things troubled him about Parker's record. Organized labor opposed the nomination because Parker had been hostile to trade unions and had endorsed "yellow dog" contracts. The most damaging blow to Parker's nomination, however, was a racist quote from the judge's past. Parker had once said, "The participation of the Negro in politics is a source of evil and danger to both races and is not desired by the wise men in either race." McNary urged Hoover to withdraw the nomination, but the president defended Parker and grumbled about his opposition. Working with the progressives, McNary helped forge the coalition that defeated Parker's nomination by two votes. The American Federation of Labor paid public tribute to McNary for his leadership in blocking Parker's appointment.

McNary and Hoover also clashed over public power. From the start of his political career, McNary had been an advocate of public ownership and operation of hydroelectric plants. "The people come first," McNary asserted, "when the ownership, development, and control of water power of the country are concerned." After a decade-long battle, McNary teamed with Senator Norris in 1931 and won Senate approval for government operation of the Muscle Shoals dam in the Tennessee Valley. "Shall a thing be done for the people," asked McNary, "or shall it be surrendered to private gain?" Hoover accused Norris and "other Socialists" of trying to drive privately owned utilities into chaos. In his veto message, Hoover said, "I am firmly opposed to the government entering into any business the major purpose of which is competition with our citizens." McNary lacked the votes to override Hoover's veto.

The political differences between McNary and Hoover finally led to deep-seated personal animosities. McNary suggested to his friend Robert S. Allen, the stocky, hard-nosed Washington bureau chief of the *Christian Science Monitor*, that he ought to investigate Hoover's finances and early business career. "Hoover poses as a great champion of the people," McNary snorted. "But he isn't a great engineer. He is a great crook." In his memoirs, Hoover denounced McNary-Haugenism as fascism and claimed that Alfred E. Smith's biggest mistake in the 1928 campaign was aligning himself with the McNary farm legislation. For the most part, McNary and Hoover kept private their mutual emnity. In his correspondence with his brother, McNary wrote disdainfully about Hoover's political and administrative capabilities. In Senate debates, McNary made no defense when Democrats and progressives blasted Hoover's policies. On the issue of relief, McNary thought Hoover was tragically wrong, a man out of step with his times.

Even so, McNary supported Hoover's re-election in 1932. Such GOP progressives as George Norris, Hiram Johnson, and Robert La Follette Jr. threw their support to Franklin D. Roosevelt. Had it not been for his leadership ambitions in the Senate, McNary might well have joined them in deserting Hoover. But McNary had come too far to forfeit his claim to his party's leadership.

McNary, Vice President
Curtis, and House Speaker
Longworth (top) joined
President Hoover for the
signing of a $500 million
farm-relief bill which the
Oregon senator had spon-
sored.

While McNary and Her-
bert Hoover had known
each other since their boyhood in Oregon, they were
never close friends and
would become bitter ad-
versaries. On this occasion
(bottom), McNary joined
the Hoovers on the presi-
dential yacht for a Potomac
cruise. (Both author's collection)

During the Hoover Administration, Senator James Watson of
Indiana held the title of majority leader, but McNary had more
influence and power. (Author's collection)

As assistant majority leader during the Hoover administration, McNary became known as the man who ran the Senate. He was among the first Senate leaders to make frequent use of the telephone in lining up votes. (Author's collection)

13
Power in the Senate

IN NOVEMBER of 1928, Charles L. McNary was widely regarded as the Senate's heir apparent. The Republican majority would soon choose a replacement for Senate Majority Leader Charles Curtis, who had just been elected vice president. Although McNary had less seniority than the two declared candidates, James Watson of Indiana and Wesley Jones of Washington, the Oregonian was more popular among his colleagues. "It is doubtful whether there is any member better liked among all classes of senators than he is," congressional correspondent Clinton W. Gilbert wrote in the *New York Post*. "Mr. McNary is one of the best politicians in the upper house. He is almost the equal of Mr. Curtis in understanding the inside politics of the Senate. He knows the motives of the individual senators better than anyone else who will be left on the floor after Mr. Curtis takes the chair. And he is a cleverer man than Mr. Curtis."

With solid progressive suppport and substantial backing from the Old Guard, McNary appeared to have the votes to claim the leadership. But when Watson and Jones persisted in their campaigns for the job, the Oregon senator decided not to run and instead sought to use his influence to settle the leadership fight without bloodletting.

"I'm trying to get the leadership fight straightened out by polls," McNary wrote Ella on 10 December, "and it is rather left to me to do so. Some of the members are insisting that I take it, but I simply cannot stand the additional work, with its worry and strain, added to the duties involved in my own committees, and then, there are those who feel they are entitled to it particularly, on account of seniority of service. I think I could have it if I wanted it, but I don't want to take on any more responsibilities at this session of Congress."

A day later, he wrote his brother: "I'm trying to compose the differences that exist between senators Watson and Jones in respect to the leadership of the Senate, but the fight is taking on some ugly aspects and I think I have arranged an agreement between them and Watson will be the leader and Jones will hold his chairmanship and be assistant leader and whip. I could have cut into this situation even though these others outranked me in service, but there are probably some sore spots and I felt I could not afford to leave the chairmanship of the Senate Committee on Agriculture and Forestry. Then I did not want to carry the additional responsibility knowing it meant nothing to my State other than a little prestige here and there."

McNary got Jones to accept his terms and the Washington senator withdrew in Watson's favor and accepted the second spot. The Oregon Republican wrote his brother that he had no regrets about not making the race himself. "I had the newspaper boys of the country solidly at my back as well wishers," wrote McNary. "But had I permitted my name to be used, it would have caused some sore spots and probably crippled my influence in the Senate."

As it happened, McNary had strengthened his hand by acting as power broker. He became chairman of the Republican Committee on Committees which he described as "a powerful political committee that assigns chairmanships and makes up the personnel of the committees." By tradition, the post had belonged to a ranking member of the Senate's inner circle. "It has been someone who has been universally admired for fairness," another senator later observed. In filling the openings on choice committees, McNary took pains to make the assignments on an equitable basis. "Reconstruction of the Senate committees," McNary wrote his brother, was "a difficult technical job requiring considerable skill and tact."

Although McNary distributed most of his plumbs on a seniority basis, he also sought ideological balance. When Senator Robert M. La Follette, Jr., applied to succeed his late father on the Finance Committee, the Old Guard and a group of newly elected conservatives known as the "Young Turks" attempted to block his appointment. The conservatives were troubled by the prospect that the progressive Wisconsin senator would eventually inherit the chairmanship of Finance. At the last minute, the Old Guard submitted the application of Senator Guy Goff of West Virginia in an obvious move to keep La Follette off the committee. Until this instance, Goff had shown little interest in tax issues. Insisting on fair play, McNary disregarded Goff's seniority and put through La Follette's appointment.

McNary soon became a figure of more consequence than the bumbling majority leader. "Sunny" Jim Watson was a throwback to the Gilded Age, a Thomas Nast cartoon sprung to life, a jowly man with a massive paunch, heavy shoulders, and small beady eyes. Watson's speeches were a spectacle of noise and bunkum. Despite the fact that he had been in Congress since 1894, Watson had yet to write any major legislation. On patronage and pork barrel grabs, he was the undisputed past master. As majority leader, he was weak and ineffective.

Like Watson, assistant leader Wesley Jones was the product of a bygone era. The Washington state Republican had launched his political career campaigning for James G. Blaine in 1884. Since his election to the Senate in 1909, Jones had become well entrenched in the Senate hierarchy and earned high marks as an advocate of regional interests. McNary struck up a friendship with Jones soon after coming to the nation's capitol and they became frequent golfing companions. Though Jones was politically to the right of McNary, the Pacific Northwest colleagues worked together on such issues as public power and farm relief. The main reason that McNary selected Watson over his friend for the majority leadership was his concern about Jones's health. Never robust, Jones looked frail and elderly. But as fate would have it, Watson's health snapped under the strain of leadership. In the fall of 1929, Watson embarked for Florida for a long convalescence.

McNary was somewhat taken aback when Wesley Jones took over Senator Watson's duties. "Most of the members of the Senate regretted that Senator Jones wanted to act as leader," McNary wrote his brother on 4 November, "and it seemed to be unanimous among the Republicans that I should take Senator Watson's place, but I said 'no, not if Senator Jones wanted it.' However, it was a good thing, because I think I would have a little too much to do, but it looks as though eventually I shall take up the leadership."

In the meantime, a revolt was brewing against the uninspired Senate leadership. Both the progressives and Young Turks called on McNary to lead the rebellion. This time, McNary was plainly interested. "Things are moving along here in a hectic sort of fashion," he reported to his brother on 18 November. "I am the recipient of an almost overwhelming temptation to take the leadership of the Senate. I could have had it for some time by the simple saying of yes, but it is a hard proposition right now, and, yet that doesn't particularly frighten me as I have a good deal of courage in that line of work. Senator Watson, the leader, is away sick. Senator Jones, assistant leader, is here, but not in the best of health and I have not the heart to be the virile actor in their overthrow."

One week later, the death of Francis E. Warren, the 85-year-old chairman of the Senate Appropriations Committee, provided McNary the opportunity he had been waiting for. Jones was next in line for this prime committee chairmanship. The Oregon senator agreed to let him have it on the condition that Jones step down as assistant leader. When Jones agreed, McNary was the overwhelming favorite to succeed him as whip.

"I may take the assistant leadership," McNary wrote his brother, "because ultimately, and probably shortly, it will lead to leadership—a position never yet filled in the Senate by a Western man. Yet I may not take it. I have not made up my mind to do so, but probably will consider it during the week. In some respects, I covet the leadership, as it brings with it many rewards for service and I'm bold enough to think I can handle the position."

So did his colleagues. Once McNary announced that he wanted the job, all opposition faded. At the party's caucus, the Oregon senator won by a unanimous vote. Despite the protest of Pennsylvania's Joseph Grundy, McNary retained the chairmanship of the Committee on Committees. "Later," McNary wrote a friend, "I shall take up the full leadership with preparation the ballplayer gets in the Minors."

McNary was being unduly modest, for most senators already viewed him as their de facto leader. While Watson made speeches, it was McNary who quietly made the Senate work. As assistant leader, McNary scheduled legislation, controlled floor debate and lined up votes on priority roll calls. "McNary has become the greatest constructive force in the Senate," a national magazine reported in May of 1930. "That is, he is the man who is getting things done. McNary does not drive, nor does he lead. He guides. And his steermanship is so gentle and deft that it is a pleasure to go along with him. The first essential of this art is the confidence of one's colleagues, which he has in abundance— from Smoot to Norris, from Glass to Wheeler, the extremes on both sides of the chamber. He gained it by 'square shooting.' When he says a thing will be done, it is done and done on time."

In soliciting the votes of his colleagues, McNary was not an armtwister. He did not threaten or cajole. The McNary treatment was subtle, low-key, and remarkably effective. "His real ability," said one Washington correspondent, "lies in knowing the man or men to pick in a pinch. He is an amateur psychologist. He knows where an emotion can be touched and aroused. He seldom asks for a vote. He merely paints the picture and lays it before the prospective voter. Senators usually elect to follow his uncanny judgement."

McNary enjoyed his new responsibilities. "I'm busy on the floor of the Senate trying to run the show and get quite a little fun out of it," he wrote his sister in April of 1930. A month later, he wrote, "I'm getting considerable pleasure out of making up the legislative program and carrying it out in the Senate. The Republican and Democratic members have been very kind to me."

A 1930 survey of Washington newspaper correspondents rated McNary as the most popular senator. "If the vote had been taken among the senators, the result would have been the same," reported *Collier's*, which depicted him as the Senate's most effective conciliator and dismissed Watson as his front man. McNary, the magazine's political columnist wrote, "cares more for personal relations than he does for policies, except in that softly and discreetly rebellious heart of his. He has more contacts than anyone else in the Senate. There is a kind of chemical substance which in the presence of two mutually hostile chemical elements promotes fusion and combination. That is what Charlie McNary is. He is the anti-knock mixture in the Senate gasoline."

Although McNary's wife suggested that he consider retiring to Fir Cone, he liked the Senate too much to give such an option serious thought. "I am not in a position to retire unless forced to by an outraged constiuency," he wrote privately. "I have nothing else to do that is exciting; certainly I would not go back to the law business. I would a whole lot rather specialize in the culture and propagation of wild geese and probably could do very much better in that field of endeavor."

His growing prominence in the Senate discouraged serious opposition to his re-election in 1930. For the first time, he went unchallenged in the Republican primary. "That is very fine as it leaves me out of considerable annoyance," McNary wrote Ella. Former Congressman Elton Watkins, a Portland Democrat, was his rival in the general election. "I know the Democratic opponent very well," McNary told his sister, "and I think I shall get along with him nicely."

McNary's attitude changed, though, when Watkins began attacking his record on public power and farm relief, disputing his credentials as a progressive. Watkins probably tarnished his own credibility by accusing McNary of being a captive of the power trust. At the time, public power was the dominant issue in Oregon politics. In the May GOP primaries, State Senator George Joseph, an outspoken advocate of public power, defeated Governor Norblad for the gubernatorial nomination. A few weeks later, Joseph suddenly died. As his replacement, the state Republican Central Committee chose Phil Metschan, owner of the Imperial Hotel, a conservative with close ties to the private utility interests. Unwilling to support Metschan, progressive Republicans nominated Portland merchant Julius Meier as an independent candidate for governor.

Not wishing to alienate either the Meier or Metschan camps, McNary declined any public comment on the gubernatorial contest. Politically, he was closer to Meier, whose campaign was managed by longtime McNary advisor Henry Hanzen. But McNary had personal ties to Metschan, who had been a boyhood friend in Salem and a classmate at Stanford. Metschan pressed hard for an endorsement from the senator. Robert C. Notson, then a young *Oregonian* reporter following the Metschan campaign, was in the lobby of a Bend hotel with his candidate when McNary suddenly entered the room. Hopeful of finally getting a commitment of support, Metschan began walking toward McNary. As soon as McNary saw what was happening, he walked out of the hotel. "There was a constant strain," McNary later wrote, "on account of the unusual situation which I did not enjoy."

On election night, McNary was among the few Republican senators to survive. The GOP's Senate majority had been slashed from an edge of 17 to 1. In the House of Representatives, the

Republican edge had been cut from 104 to 3. McNary's vote more than doubled Watkins and swept every county in Oregon. "The vote I received was splendid—unusual under the circumstances," he wrote his brother. As for Watkins, McNary added, "I did not relish being abused or misrepresented by a skunk, but his overwhelming defeat was a pleasurable reward." In the governor's race, Meier won by a handsome margin.

In the wake of the GOP's overwhelming defeat in the 1930 midterm elections, the Senate progressives made a renewed effort to out Watson as majority leader. They also sought the removal of New Hampshire's flinty George H. Moses as president pro tempore. McNary was the only name seriously mentioned as Watson's replacement. For weeks, there had been speculation that the Oregon senator would finally make his move. McNary's supporters came up with a plan that would have made Watson president pro tempore and McNary majority leader. Hoover liked the idea of dumping Watson, who he described as having "spasmodic loyalties and abilities." But not with McNary. The President termed the Oregon senator "a shade too radical," and the *New York Times* later reported that Hoover had effectively vetoed McNary's promotion to majority leader. "Hoover's prize congressional mistake," wrote Douglas Gilbert in the *New York World Telegram*, "was to thumb down the movement to make McNary Republican floor leader. It would have been a marvelous coup since McNary is on the best of terms with the progressive group—Borah, La Follette, Norris, and Cutting—while also enjoying the trust and respect of the Democrats. But McNary lost out. The President, feeling that if he consented to the move, he would be playing ball with the progressives, refused his sanction. And nothing will be accomplished—for Hoover personally—in the Congress because the step was not taken that would have harmonized to some extent anyway, its factions."

Had McNary announced his candidacy for majority leader, the White House could not have prevented his election. But Hoover's opposition could have dimmed his enthusiasm for making the race. McNary told his brother it was his decision not to run. "I did not have the heart to interfere with Senator Watson's position," he wrote, "though a willing word would have performed the act." He added, "As Senator Watson has a campaign on in the spring, I told the boys I should be happy to have him serve."

McNary told the insurgents that it was not worth the trouble to oust Moses. "It is an unimportant position," he wrote his brother. McNary, however, was unable to hold back a challenge. Both Arthur Vandenberg, a Michigan Republican, and Key Pittman, a Nevada Democrat, ran against Moses. When none of the candidates could manage a majority in 23 ballots, Moses kept the title under an old rule that the incumbent retained office until a successor was elected.

Without a working majority, McNary found the going much tougher in 1931. But he helped Hoover gain approval of the Reconstruction Finance Corporation, an agency that was soon making government loans to banks, railroads, insurance companies, and farm mortgage associations. He also lined up support for the Glass-Steagall Act which made $750 million available for business and industry. McNary backed the Democratic Wagner-Garner bill which would have provided direct relief for the unemployed and public works jobs. Although it passed both houses, Hoover vetoed the measure.

Even so, McNary held out hope that Hoover would agree to other relief measures. The Oregon senator sponsored legislation authorizing the distribution of surplus wheat to the hungry. "I do not know what the president will do," he admitted, "but it is my judgment he will carry out any orders contained in a statute enacted by Congress. There is no way to establish that fact except to present the resolution for his signature. In my heart and in my opinion, if he still believes it is in the interest of those in distress, he will properly function under the resolution."

When McNary's resolution passed, however, Hoover refused to make the grain available. More and more, the Oregon Republican was running out of patience with Hoover's rigid ideology. McNary cooperated with Democrats and progressives on other anti-depression measures. Drew Pearson and Robert Allen reported that McNary bristled when conservative GOP colleagues Arthur Vandenberg and Simeon Fess demanded that he shelve a Democratic bill. As the two senators finished making their pitch, McNary stood and shook his fist in their faces. "You voted billions for the banks, for the railroads, for the insurance companies," he said, "and now when it is proposed to give the starving little fellow a few pennies, you want the bill killed. You get the hell out of here." Vandenberg and Fess did just that.

As McNary had warned, Hoover's doctrinaire policies reinforced the widely held view that his Republican administration was insensitive to the plight of the poor. Hoover had also managed to alienate much of the GOP's middle class political base. When the president campaigned, he was frequently booed. Franklin D. Roosevelt, the Democratic nominee, blamed Hoover for the Depression and, at the same time, offered hope that a new administration could do something about it. On 8 November 1932, Roosevelt won in a landslide. "It is all over including the shocking," McNary wrote his brother, "and I really was surprised at the extent of the Democratic victory. Repeatedly I said that in my opinion Governor Roosevelt had the edge and stood the best chance to win the contest, but I still could not remove from the back of my head the fact that for the last three presidential campaigns, the Republicans had a majority of about seven million."

This majority turned out to be Roosevelt's winning margin over Hoover. The Democrats also gained control of the Senate in the FDR sweep. Among the most prominent Republican casualties were senators Watson, Moses and Jones, which left McNary as the sole surviving member of the leadership. Under the circumstances, McNary felt fortunate that he had not been up for re-election. "I just had a conference with Senator Watson," McNary wrote a friend, "poor fellow looks a little bit whipped after so many years of public life, losing his state by over 250,000. Every pitcher goes to the well once too often, so do many prizefighters, and public officials enter the arena once too often."

Over the next four months, the GOP retained nominal control of the Senate during the "lame duck" session before the new Congress was seated. Although Watson turned over the leadership to McNary, there was little that could be done during the interval before FDR's inauguration. The Democratic and progressive Republican senators awaited direction from the new administration. As the economy took a turn for the worse and the lines of unemployed workers grew even longer, McNary still found Hoover reluctant to do much. "You can get nothing by Mr. Hoover at this time," McNary wrote in January of 1933, noting that the president had been "deeply stung by his defeat."

At the end of the session, McNary's Republican colleagues presented him with a handsome silver tray inscribed as "a slight token of their appreciation for his ability, his devotion and loyalty to his country and his courtesy and many kindnesses to them individually." When the senator's cousin Carlton Savage asked McNary how he built such rapport with all factions of his party, the Oregonian replied, "I always keep my word."

With his party no longer controlling the Senate, McNary had to give up the chairmanship of the Agricultural Committee. "That's a part of the ever changing political game," he wrote privately. McNary, though, was one of the few Republicans who could find a silver lining in the party's defeat. By a unanimous vote, he was chosen as Senate minority leader. And, now that there was a Democratic president, Charles L. McNary suddenly found himself the highest ranking Republican officeholder in the land. "That will be some compensation," he told John McNary, "for the losses I suffered in the change of political forces."

This is how Jo Metzer of the *Philadelphia Inquirer* portrayed the newly elected Senate minority leader in February of 1933. (Author's collection)

JUST ONE SNOWFALL AFTER ANOTHER!

As the nation's highest-ranking Republican officeholders, Senate Minority Leader McNary and House Minority Leader Bertrand Snell of New York were their party's most visible spokesmen during FDR's first term. (This page and opposite page, top.)

ASSET OR LIABILITY?

While Democratic National Chairman James A. Farley's praise may have helped McNary among Democrats and independents (bottom), it certainly did not enhance his image among Republican conservatives. (Four C. K. Berryman cartoons. All author's collection)

Floor leaders of their respective parties, McNary and Joseph Robinson of Arkansas (top) had a close working relationship; the Oregon senator said they were "as close as two brothers."

The subtle McNary (below) had little use for the overheated rhetoric of the Senate's orators. (Both author's collection)

14

The Loyal Opposition

SENATOR McNary was among the few Republicans whose national stature had been enhanced by the coming of the New Deal. "My party responsibilities will be considerably larger than they have been inasmuch as we shall have no president," McNary told his sister. On 7 March 1933, the thirty-six Republican senators unanimously chose McNary as Senate minority leader and chairman of the Republican Conference. Sixteen years after his appointment to the Senate, McNary was the chief spokesman for his party, the leader of the opposition. McNary told his sister that the floor leadership was "a position which I have wanted for some time and which satisfies me from the viewpoint of political power and precedent."

His most difficult task was to try to keep the Old Guard and progressive factions of the party from fighting each other. At McNary's first caucus as minority leader, he thwarted a move by Pennsylvania conservative David Reed to purge from their committees the four Republican mavericks who had supported Roosevelt over Hoover. "All Republicans look alike to me," McNary declared.

His elevation to the floor leadership brought McNary more attention than anything in his public career. *U.S. News* described him as "the perfect parliamentarian," "the finest mind since Lodge," the Senate's "most brilliant strategist." A leading Washington columnist explained that McNary "is gifted with perhaps the finest political mind that the Senate has known since the passing of Nelson W. Aldrich," the dominant senator of Theodore Roosevelt's era. In a thumbnail sketch, the *New York American* described McNary: "Of medium height, slender and even boyish-looking in figure, graceful in his movements, and reminding one somewhat of a humming-bird, as he flits silently in and out of the Senate."

The *Saturday Evening Post*'s Samuel G. Blythe drew a similar portrait: "McNary is also everybody's friend. They all like him. He doesn't bother much about making speeches, but can make a good one if he wants to, and spends his time moving about. He is just under sixty, a ruddy-faced, confidential sort of a fellow, who can wander over to the Democratic side and get anything he wants within reason from his opponents, and sometimes without reason."

McNary's intimate friendships with the Democratic leadership, which he had cultivated for more than a decade, added to his effectiveness as Minority Leader. During the 1920s he had become so close to Democratic floor leader Joseph T. Robinson that McNary was often admitted, as a friend, to the Arkansas senator's Capital hideaway for noon strategy meetings with Pat Harrison of Mississippi and Claude Swanson of Virginia. Now, Robinson was the majority leader and with his new title came authority. Robinson was his party's strongest leader in the Senate, a bullish autocrat with a booming voice and sharp temper. For punching out another member, Robinson once lost his membership in a fashionable Washington country club. Through force of personality, Robinson pushed through the Democratic caucus a rule that made causus decisions on New Deal bills binding by majority vote. Badly outnumbered, McNary could seldom defeat Robinson in a showdown. So he relied on behind-the-scenes negotiations with his friend. "Charley always sized up people and he didn't wade into a tough guy and try to be tougher," Robert S. Allen recalled years later. "He played on Joe Robinson's foibles."

During the turbulent first "Hundred Days" of the Roosevelt administration, McNary ardently backed most of the New Deal measures, agreeing with Roosevelt that the national emergency required extraordinary action. McNary supported the Emergency Banking Act, which passed both houses of Congress in eight hours and provided for reopening the nation's banks. He took a leading role in the passage of the Tennessee Valley Authority Act, and the cause that he had been fighting so many years with George Norris became reality. McNary opposed the Federal Emergency Relief Act which went beyond his own concept of direct relief assistance. Not suprisingly, he gave strong support to the Agricultural Adjustment Act, the bold farm relief plan that had evolved from the principles of McNary-Haugenism. McNary termed the National Recovery bill "the most important proposal that has ever been presented to this or any other Congress" and he worked for its quick passage. Designed to revive industry and reduce unemployment, the National Industrial Recovery Act (NRA) applied "codes" to some seven hundred industries, which included the setting of minimum wage and maximum hour regulations. Under the NRA, industry reabsorbed four million unemployed workers. The recovery act also established the Public Works Administration with more than three billion dollars to put the unemployed to work on a massive construction program of roads, bridges, public buildings, and other projects. When the special congressional session adjourned in June, all of Roosevelt's fifteen major proposals had been adopted and the whirlwind pace of the "Hundred Days" left McNary exhausted. "Congress days are over," McNary wrote Ella, "and I feel as if I had suddenly been released from prison."

In the closing moments of the historic session, Majority Leader Robinson praised McNary's constructive leadership and cooperation. Actually, McNary agreed in principle with more of the New Deal than the conservative Robinson, who had opposed public power and feared the NRA labor codes, and more than once he comforted the majority leader when Robinson found it gnawing to push through an administration program. McNary admired Robinson's party loyalty and his effectiveness, yet he privately lectured his friend for his tactless habit of rebuking Democratic followers on the Senate floor. Because of their long friendship, the two leaders confided in each other freely and without inhibitions.

As minority leader, McNary commanded the respect of Democratic senators and it was not unusual for colleagues to come across the aisle and seek his opinion on legislation. McNary did his best to be of assistance. In 1933, courtly, soft-spoken freshman Senator Richard B. Russell of Georgia turned to McNary for help in handling the administration's agricultural appropriation bill. "I was a new senator, without experience in handling such complicated measures," Russell said years later.

"Though he was a member of a different political party, I went to Senator McNary before opening hearings on the bill to seek the benefit of his advice and counsel. He could not have been kindlier or more cooperative had I been not only a member of his party but an intimate friend or relative." Within a short time, Russell was making use of McNary's knowledge in other legislative areas. "For ten years I leaned heavily on him," said Russell, "and he gave freely of his great ability and rich experience."

From his years as assistant majority leader, McNary knew the strengths and weaknesses of his Republican followers. He understood a senator's drive and motivation, his flexibility, his favorite issues and pork barrel projects, the politics of his state, and the pressure groups he needed to please. Whenever something of interest to a Republican senator was coming up, McNary made certain that his colleague knew about it. With fewer committee slots available in a Democratic Senate, McNary had the difficult task of rearranging committee assignments and bumping some colleagues from important committees. In reassigning senators, McNary tried to accommodate their interests. When Senator Cutting had to be moved from Foreign Relations, a prime committee, McNary arranged for the New Mexico senator's transfer to Agriculture and Irrigation, committees that were of much importance to Cutting's state. Such patronage gave McNary considerable influence and, as in the past, he won high marks for his fairness.

McNary disappointed his party's hard-liners, who wanted him to be more of a demagogue in his criticism of the New Deal. Senators Reed and Vandenberg pressed for reactionary opposition, arguing that it was the duty of Republicans to oppose. Once again, McNary aligned himself with the insurgents against the party militants. "In times of depression," said McNary, "party politics should be put aside."

Sometimes McNary complained about the frustrations of trying to be all things to his followers. "I'll be d-—if I am not getting tired of politics," he wrote John in December of 1933, "especially the kind I am having to go through—Leading the Minority and the so-called candidate in '36, a link between the Progressives and the Stand-patters, criticized by some for being too close to the President, by others for being too friendly toward the Conservatives and by some for being too friendly toward the Progressives. I really present a picture no artist can paint and it's deucedly trying."

Whatever the difficulties of his balancing act, McNary cherished his position as first among thirty-six Republican equals. The trappings of power included a one-room Capitol "hideaway" with elaborate rococo architecture and nineteenth-century European art; the opulent minority leader's suite in the Senate Office Building with a magnificent terrace and a commanding view of the Potomac River, the Washington Monument, the Lincoln Memorial, the Capitol, and the Lee mansion at Arlington; and his minority conference committee room with fourteen-foot French mirrors, spectacular crystal chandeliers, twenty-foot ceiling, and lush deep green carpeting. "You will have to see this room to enjoy its beauty," McNary told his sister, noting that it was "the largest and most handsome room in the building." In McNary's private office, a modest room with a marble fireplace, chandelier, and huge window, were photographs of Fir Cone, Crater Lake, and Mount Hood. Although he talked wistfully of his future retirement in Oregon, McNary had never been more comfortable in the nation's capitol.

McNary and his daughter Charlotte, Washington, D.C., 1935.
(Author's collection)

15

McNary and Roosevelt

IT WAS ONE of the most remarkable political alliances in American history, an unprecedented relationship between a president and the leader of the opposition party. They put aside political differences in an effort to bring an end to the nation's worst depression. In the process, Franklin Delano Roosevelt and Charles Linza McNary built a lasting friendship. "The victory was rather larger than I expected," McNary wrote Ella following FDR's election in 1932, "but inasmuch as it had to be, I'm rather glad that it was overwhelming. It may cause an upturn in business."

Even though the two men had been on the national political scene since the Wilson Administration, they did not meet until five weeks before FDR's inauguration. The Democratic president-elect told McNary of his plans to seek emergency measures, and the Oregon Republican pledged his support. "He is very affable and I think very much on the square," McNary wrote his brother, "and I am sure it will be a pleasure to work with him."

After the frustration of dealing with conservative ideologues Hoover and Coolidge, McNary liked having a president who was politically flexible and more interested in results than philosophical purity. Roosevelt and McNary were pragmatists who believed that politics was the art of the possible. "A master politician," was McNary's early appraisal of FDR. Both men had experienced political defeat in their first statewide primary campaigns and had shown the resourcefulness to come back. Roosevelt valued McNary's judgement and his shrewd political instincts. When they had disagreements, the two men respected each other's views and would not let honest differences of opinion sour their relationship. Indeed, FDR appreciated McNary's frank criticism and his low-key, yet biting wit. One of the qualities that the Oregon Republican most admired was FDR's patrician sense of noblesse oblige, his devotion to the common people, and his refusal to let political and governmental traditions stand in the way of helping the victims of the Depression.

Shortly before Roosevelt took office, McNary called for bold measures to lift the nation out of the crisis. "We know that wealth is not secure while labor wants, finding no outlet for legitimate use of brain and brawn," he said, "that a high standard of American manhood and womanhood cannot be assured when hundreds of thousands of our children are ill-nourished, or wandering homeless through the land."

Roosevelt was fully aware of the urgency of the moment. Many of the nation's banks had closed that winter and the ranks of the jobless had grown into the millions. When a friend told FDR that his success would earn him a place in history as the greatest American president and that failure could tarnish him as the worst, Roosevelt solemnly replied, "If I fail, I shall be the last one."

Henry A. Wallace, the Iowa farm editor who would soon become FDR's secretary of agriculture, said years later that he had heard disturbing reports that the Army felt it might have to take over the government to prevent a revolution. Senator David Reed, a conservative Republican from Pennsylvania, said in the winter of 1933, "If this country ever needed a Mussolini, it needs one now."

FDR's inaugural address was positively electrifying. In a strong, confident voice, he declared "The only thing we have to fear is fear itself." Roosevelt served notice that he would stop at nothing to lead the nation through the Depression. If required, he said, "I shall ask Congress for the one remaining instrument to meet the crisis: broad executive power to wage a war against the emergency as great as the power that would be given to me if we were in fact invaded by a foreign foe."

At the conclusion of his remarks, Roosevelt sent word for McNary and Senator James Couzens of Michigan to meet with him in the President's Room just inside the Capitol. When the

Oregon senator arrived, FDR greeted him warmly and then asked for his cooperation in pushing through his cabinet appointments and anti-depression measures. Without hesitation, McNary pledged his help. "I will get along with him," McNary told *Oregon Journal* correspondent Carl Smith following this meeting.

Five days after taking the oath of office, Roosevelt called Congress into special session. With McNary's backing, the president gained passage of his Emergency Banking Relief Act on the same day it was submitted to Capitol Hill. The nation's banks were closed and in FDR's first fireside chat, he announced over the radio that he was reopening them, and millions of Americans started putting their money back in the banks. McNary, who preferred public works jobs to the dole, actively supported the Civil Works Administration, which would put more than four million Americans back to work over the next year. He also backed the Civilian Conservation Corps that provided jobs for 250,000 young men in planting trees, fighting forest fires, and building dams and other projects. The Congress approved an appropriation of $500 million for direct relief payments to the states. The Farm Credit Administration and Home Owners Loan Corporation were established to help stem the tide of depression foreclosures. McNary worked with Wallace and Rexford G. Tugwell, the New Deal brain truster in negotiations over the Agriculture Adjustment Act that increased the purchasing power of farmers, and raised the ceiling for farm loans by banks. "McNary was more of a New Deal radical than most of the New Dealers and the so-called Senate progressives," Tugwell recalled in 1974. "He was always fair-minded and did his homework. McNary was my idea of what a good senator should be." Tugwell said that Roosevelt's commitment to farm relief was what firmly cemented his political alliance with the Oregon senator. "Roosevelt came along," said Tugwell, "and gave McNary what he had wanted for years—parity for the farmers."

McNary had friendly ties with many of the New Dealers. The secretary of agriculture, Henry A. Wallace, was the son and namesake of McNary's late political ally, Secretary Henry C. Wallace, who had held the same office in the Harding Administration. Young Henry, as the editor of *Wallace's Farmer*, had been a leading proponent of McNary-Haugenism. Interior Secretary Harold Ickes, like McNary, had been a progressive Republican and was a staunch conservationist. McNary took an immediate liking to Ickes, who was known as the "old cur-mudgeon." Secretary of State Cordell Hull, a Southern gentle-man of the old school, had been one of McNary's favorite Sen-ate colleagues. Hull's closest aide was Carlton Savage, McNary's cousin, an idealistic and scholarly young man who had left a college faculty to come to Washington and had written a two-volume history of American maritime policy in time of war that had earned critical praise from FDR.

Roosevelt's fast start gave McNary hope. "Everyone here is more or less optimistic concerning the future," he wrote in April, "and I think out of this legislation Congress has passed at the suggestion of the new President, that benefits nationwide will ensue." A month later, he reported, "The President seem-ingly has gotten away to a good start and really I think condi-tions are better than they were and will improve."

"For the present, politics is in a state of coma," McNary said when Congress adjourned in the summer of 1933. "Every good citizen believes President Roosevelt should have a fair and full opportunity to administer the laws and exercise the power which Congress gave unto him. In my opinion the members of the Republican party do not desire to bait and badger the Presi-dent, or if he should fail in his administration, to provide him with any alibis. During the last session of Congress, I cooper-ated with the President in the preparation and achievement of his program, as I believed in putting public welfare above any other consideration. To oppose the President now in a purely partisan spirit would be rocking the boat at a particularly un-fortunate time."

McNary commended FDR's leadership. "Our country is on the upgrade," he said. "Industries of every kind are feeling the impulse of better times. The program of President Roosevelt supported by the Congress has inspired confidence and cour-age, and doubt has given way to doing."

Later in the summer, the Senate minority leader quietly be-gan selling FDR on his proposal for a government-built dam on the Columbia river at Bonneville. On 30 August 1933, McNary wrote the president that the great dam was "a subject close to my heart." The senator added, "This development would mark the first step in the complete utilization of this great river for navigation, flood control and erosion with a wholesome quan-tity of electrical power as an incident thereto. Most pleasantly I recall in conversations with you that we shared the mutual belief that this project would be undertaken under the Public Works Act."

A few days later, McNary was advised that the Roosevelt Administration was considering a scaled-down version of his proposal. Though Roosevelt had given McNary his support for Bonneville Dam, there was much competition for the huge sums that had been allocated to the Public Works Administration. The private power interests were fighting McNary's proposal for transmission lines to cities and public cooperatives. Sensing that the federal dam might be in jeopardy, Congressman Charles H. Martin of Portland asked McNary to head back for Washington and personally confront FDR.

"Without delay I hastened to Washington," McNary recalled, "where I met General Martin and we called on the President and urged the allocation of public works funds for the construction of the Bonneville project. The President thought that the project should be further surveyed and explored. I told him that this had been done by the Army Engineers and they had reported favorably. After much discussion and some urging, the President said he thought allocation funds might be made, but wanted us to see Secretary Ickes. This we did, and later twenty million dollars was allocated for the commencement of the project."

Once Roosevelt got behind McNary's project, he became its chief lobbyist. The president enlisted the support of Congressman Sam Rayburn of Texas, who was then chairman of the Interstate and Foreign Commerce Committee. FDR also lined up the support of other key congressional Democrats, which assured its passage. When Roosevelt signed the Bonneville legislation, he explained to McNary's colleagues, "I've got to give Charlie his dam."

Over the next decade, Roosevelt and McNary, working with Secretary Ickes, set in motion plans for federal dams at other sites on the Columbia. The Grand Coulee project in Central Washington was the largest man-made structure in the world when it was completed in 1941. In his diary, Ickes gave McNary the credit for persuading Roosevelt and congressional leaders to undertake the Columbia Basin projects. "Senator McNary appears to have all of the northwestern senators eating out of his hand, regardless of party," observed Ickes.

Thomas C. Corcoran, FDR's close aide, said that McNary and the president were skilled professionals with a keen understanding of the nuances of politics. "McNary was a smart cookie," said Corcoran. "He knew what he wanted and played ball with Roosevelt, making it clear that he'd scratch Roosevelt's back if the president would return the favor." Henry Cabot Lodge, Jr., McNary's Republican colleague, added, "I never could see that Roosevelt took advantage of the situation to push Senator McNary, although he may have tried. Senator McNary was pretty hard to push."

There were areas of disagreement between FDR and McNary. In 1934, the Oregon Republican voted against the administration's Gold Reserve Act that lowered the dollar's value in gold and set the price of gold at thirty-five dollars an ounce. With the other western progressives, McNary opposed FDR's efforts to secure tariff-making powers for himself. The Oregon senator denounced the proposed Reciprocal Trade Agreements Act as harmful to American agriculture. The legislation gave the administration the power to reduce the tariff by half with foreign countries in exchange for reciprocal concessions on American products. McNary could not find the votes to block Roosevelt's trade bill, and it passed by a comfortable margin.

McNary resisted conservative pressure to blast Roosevelt's domestic policies. When a group of party stalwarts led by former Secretary of the Treasury Odgen Mills drafted an anti-New Deal manifesto, McNary refused to give it official sanction. The Senate minority leader argued that Republicans should offer forward-looking programs instead of reactionary bombast.

In the 1934 midterm elections, McNary and former president Hoover clashed over their party's campaign strategy. Hoover wanted nothing less than an indictment of the New Deal. McNary argued that a negative campaign would be counterproductive. While the Oregon Republican was the party's chief spokesman on Capitol Hill, Hoover's forces prevailed in maintaining their control of the Republican National Committee. A wealthy Pennsylvania conservative, Henry P. Fletcher, a Hoover loyalist, was installed that spring as GOP national chairman. Fletcher blasted Congress as nothing more than a rubber stamp for the White House. With Hoover and Fletcher launching a free-swinging assault on FDR, McNary took little part in the fall campaign. The former president urged voters to preserve the Constitution by throwing out New Deal congressmen. His new book *The Challenge to Liberty*, argued that the choice facing Americans was between "national regimentation" and "liberty."

McNary thought Hoover's efforts were anything but helpful for Republican candidates. "I wish his sentences were not so ponderous and his ideas so heavily obscured by words," he wrote a Senate colleague. "Probably he will join the American Liberty League." The organization to which McNary referred was a right-wing fringe group that drew support from wealthy businessmen.

In November, McNary's call for moderation was vindicated. Although the party holding the White House always lost congressional seats in the midterm elections, the Democrats broke that tradition in gaining ten seats in the Senate and nineteen in the House of Representatives. Senators Reed of Pennsylvania and Fess of Ohio, who were close allies of Hoover, both lost their bids for another term.

A month after the election, McNary broke his silence and denounced the rigid dogma that the former president had espoused on the campaign trail and in his recently published book. "The Republican Party should quit its abstractions and alarms and get down to the level of human sympathy and human understanding," declared the Senate minority leader. "It should now be plain that a party cannot gain the attention of a people distraught by business and employment worries by extolling the nobility of the forefathers, the sanctity of the Constitution and by spreading alarms over regimentation and bureaucracy.

"Regimentation," McNary continued, "is a fine, mouth-filling word, but it fills no empty stomachs, and a man who is worried over where next month's rent is coming from cannot be aroused to an interest in the evils of bureaucracy."

Because of the depression, the Oregon senator said that Republicans had a special responsibility to join forces with the Democratic administration "to rescue the country." Roosevelt welcomed McNary's pledge of continued cooperation. "He is a lovely fellow," McNary wrote his brother in January of 1935, "I have always liked him and we get along splendidly, so much better than I did with the forgotten man, Mr. Hoover."

McNary was disappointed when FDR reacted sharply to Democratic opposition to the prevailing wage provision of the administration's relief bill. "The President has lost considerable of his influence with his party and has developed recently a rather childish peevishness, which should not be the part of a big fellow," McNary wrote his brother on February 26, 1935. "I have supported the program loyally and helped him in many ways on the work relief bill but because he lost by one vote on the prevailing wage provision he hoisted the white flag and ran away like a child, but in my opinion we will pass it a little later."

In the end, FDR got nearly everything he asked for. McNary was a leading supporter of Roosevelt's most enduring legacy, the Social Security Act, which provided unemployment compensation and a pension for the elderly, funded from taxes on both employers and employees. The Oregon Republican also backed the Emergency Relief Appropriations Act that replaced the dole with jobs for millions of the unemployed. As McNary predicted, a security wage based on the prevailing hourly rate eventually won congressional approval. McNary voted for the Wagner Act, which created a National Labor Relations Board with collective bargaining powers and which upheld the right of employees to join trade unions. He supported the Securities and Exchange Commission that regulated financiers and the Holding Company Act that broke up the private power monopolies and restricted the power interests to localized operations.

McNary's special relationship with Roosevelt proved to be helpful in getting federal funding for construction of bridges, schools, hospitals, and other projects back home in Oregon. When the state capitol building was destroyed by fire in April 1935, McNary came up with public works money for a brand new building. Another monument to McNary's clout was Timberline Lodge, a magnificent structure built by the Works Progress Administration on the slopes of Mount Hood.

On a western campaign swing, Democratic National Chairman James A. Farley acknowledged that McNary was revered by the president. "Senator McNary is more a patriot than a partisan," Farley explained. In a 1974 interview, Farley recalled, "McNary was quite generous to Mr. Roosevelt. Instead of obstructing our programs, he did everything he could to help. Mr. Roosevelt would frequently ask him to help fill appointments to agencies like the Federal Power Commission and Interstate Commerce Commission."

When the economy was slow to respond to Roosevelt's recovery measures, McNary privately wondered if the New Deal should be modified. "I think he is going too far and too fast and probably without proper thought," he confided to his brother. McNary wrote Senator Couzens, "I find here the same unrest and feeling of uncertainty that I feel I obtained in the past. I wish the president would make a statement concerning his program so that business could adjust itself thereto. I think he could say, 'This is my program and only a great emergency will cause me to add a chapter.'"

By the summer of 1935, McNary felt it was time to become more assertive in his role as party spokesman. He publicly suggested that FDR give the country a breathing spell and focus his energies on existing programs instead of seeking more. "The emotionalism which always accompanies a political upheaval has subsided," McNary declared on 15 July. "There has been tangible improvement in the country's economic structure, but confidence is lacking throughout the land. The administration would have achieved more had it conceived less. Simply it has been going in too many places. Indisputably, the continuance of the New Deal is dependent upon its wise administration of the super-abundant powers conferred by Congress."

McNary and his wife adopted a baby girl, Charlotte, in 1935, and the senator loved being a father. Before heading for the Capitol, McNary enjoyed taking his daughter in a stroller for a morning walk along Connecticut Avenue. The president dropped Charlotte a note, confiding that she was "a very lucky little girl," and Eleanor Roosevelt sent her flowers. Robert S. Allen recalled, "Charley was absolutely crazy about his little girl." Cornelia had hoped that McNary's new responsibilities as a father might be an incentive for him to give up politics, but he was not letting the Senate interfere with parenthood and had no plans of retirement.

In looking ahead to the 1936 elections, McNary said that Republicans should not revert to their old role of being "aginners," but should offer constructive programs of their own. McNary was regarded as a possible contender for the presidential nomination. Early in his term, FDR had told a Boston political reporter that McNary would be his rival in 1936. While not enthusiastic about the prospect, Herbert Hoover admitted that McNary had the stuff to be a serious contender for the White House. As early as 1933, leading political columnists were describing the Oregon senator as presidential timber. *Newsweek* reported that GOP leaders spoke of McNary "as the one man who may unite the party and, perhaps, become its 1936 presidential candidate." Mark Sullivan wrote that McNary's nomination would unify the party more successfully than any other possibility. Another leading political analyst, Raymond

Clapper, added, "If President Roosevelt retains any large share of his popularity until 1936—Senator McNary, rather than some hair-tearing critic of everything the administration has done, will be one of the most logical persons to carry the Republican presidential standard." Alice Roosevelt Longworth, though a McNary friend, claimed that the Oregon senator's support of the New Deal had eliminated him as a convincing alternative to FDR.

The other likely Republican hopefuls included senators Vandenberg of Michigan and Borah of Idaho, and Governor Alf M. Landon of Kansas. Getting the nomination in such a field would not be easy and McNary was aware of the difficulty. He also thought FDR was in such a strong position that the Republican nomination might not be worth much. The most compelling reason why McNary passed up a national campaign in 1936 was that he was up for re-election in Oregon and that took priority over all other considerations.

Senator Couzens attempted to change McNary's mind and offered to contribute $100,000 in order to launch his presidential campaign. While they were having lunch in the Senate dining room, McNary scribbled his answer on the back of a menu:

> The presidential bee is a deadly bug
> I've seen it work on others.
> Oh Lord, protect me from its hug
> And let it sting my brothers.

Presiding over a 1936 Senate hearing on his proposals for Columbia River dams to generate hydroelectric power. (Author's collection)

McNary's longtime administrative assistant was Helen Kiefer (top).

Following Robinson's death, his successor as senate majority leader was Alben Barkley of Kentucky (bottom left). Barkley said that he and McNary developed a special bond on their discovery that their grandfathers had been born and reared within five miles of each other in North Carolina. (Both author's collection)

16

Squeaking Through

HAVING WATCHED so many of his colleagues lose their re-election bids, Senator McNary took nothing for granted about his own chances in 1936. "I would not relish getting into a primary or election fight," he wrote his brother in January. "This would be very distasteful and I might fall by the roadside in either contest."

Although McNary was approaching his sixty-second birthday and had been in the Senate for twenty years, he never seriously considered not making another race. When several challengers emerged back home, he promptly announced that he was running for re-election. "There seems to be no other course for me to pursue," he wrote John in mid-February. "I shall treat the situation philosophically and abide by the results uncomplainingly. I cannot expect to remain in public life always, nor should I." A few days later, he added, "I couldn't retire in the presence of a threat of Townsendism and would rather be a martyr and take a licking than be a cowardly dilettante, so let come what may and it will be perfectly all right with me."

The political "threat" was very real. McNary's home state had become a stronghold for supporters of an old-age pension scheme advocated by Dr. Francis E. Townsend, an elderly California physician. Townsend's plan called for a national sales tax which would provide the funding for a two hundred dollar monthly pension for everyone over sixty years of age. The only ground rule was that those receiving the pension would retire from their jobs and spend their check each month to help stimulate the economy and lift the nation out of the Depression. On a visit to the United States, British statesman Winston Churchill quipped, "The Townsend plan is an attempt to mint the moonlight into silver and coin the sunshine into gold." Economists pointed out that Townsend's plan would require half the national income and double the amount spent on all state, local, and federal taxes.

So many of the nation's elderly had lost their jobs, savings, and homes in the Depression that they rallied behind Townsend. Almost overnight, the Townsend clubs built a national membership in the millions. Some political observers wrote that Townsendites were the dominant voting bloc in no less than ten states. Oregon merchants and newspapers opposing the Townsend plan were threatened with boycotts. An Oregon state legislator, Howard Merriam, who criticized Townsendism, was recalled from office. Portland's Republican congressman W.A. Ekwall was considered vulnerable in 1936 because of his opposition to the Townsend plan. The state's two other congressmen, James Mott and Walter Pierce, embraced the doctor's Depression panacea. "I have never seen anything like the Townsend old-age pension propaganda," McNary wrote his brother in 1935. "It has reached the point that it is practically hysteria in Oregon and has attracted the favor of vast numbers of people."

McNary, however, was not buying the propaganda, which he viewed as a cruel hoax on the elderly. "I have not descended to the low down position of making promises for votes," he wrote his sister. "I suppose they will have a primary candidate and he may carry along enough votes to win and that will probably be the best thing in the world for all concerned."

His renomination, it turned out, was challenged by two supporters of the Townsend plan. Theodore Nelson, a Salem farmer and a founding member of the Townsend clubs, was the officially slated candidate of the Townsend Congressional District boards of Oregon. McNary's other primary opponent, State Senator Sam H. Brown of Gervais, was a political gadfly. Two years earlier, Brown had campaigned for the governorship as a public-power candidate, finishing second in the Republican primary. In the spring of 1936, Brown was purporting to be the old people's champion.

Confident that his two primary opponents would split less than half of the vote, McNary rejected suggestions that he raise funds for a major statewide advertising campaign. Had there been just one challenger, McNary would have been much more concerned. The senator knew what he was talking about. On 15 May, McNary swept every county in the state, finishing ahead of Brown by 67,000 votes. Between them, Brown and Nelson had received 37 percent of the Republican vote, which indicated that McNary's re-election in November was far from certain.

His opponent in the general election was Mayor Willis E. Mahoney of Klamath Falls, a spellbinding orator who had built a statewide image as a champion of the have-nots of the Depression. Twenty years younger than McNary, the Democratic Senate candidate was a fresh new face in Oregon politics. Mahoney, a native of Idaho, had been speaker of the Washington state house of representatives before moving to Klamath Falls, Oregon in the early months of the Depression. As mayor he had wiped out the city's debt by imposing heavier taxes on local utility companies. In 1934 he had made a strong but losing bid for the Democratic gubernatorial nomination, jolting the state's conservative establishment with his tax-the-rich platform. Mahoney, who had been active in Huey Long's "Share the Wealth" movement, joined forces with the Townsendites in 1936. Announcing his candidacy for the U.S. Senate at a Democratic Party dinner in the Portland Hotel, Mahoney told party activists that their biggest problem in unseating McNary was their "defeatist attitude." In the midst of cheers, a Democratic official, Warren Erwin, shouted, "I have just heard the voice of a Moses crying in the wilderness; the only man in Oregon who can defeat McNary."

With tent-preacher charisma, Mahoney charged that Senator McNary had fallen out of touch with Oregon. Palmer Hoyt of the *Oregonian* recalled that Mahoney would invariably ask if anyone in the audience had "seen the senior senator?" More often than not, nobody in the crowd had seen McNary in years. Mahoney also whipped up his audiences with emotional rhetoric, suggesting that there were solutions to the Depression's seemingly insoluble problems.

"Willis brought something to Oregon that people hadn't seen before," recalled Herbert Lundy, who was then a young Portland journalist. "It was a version of old-time Populism with some of the ideas of the Wisconsin progressives."

That summer, Mahoney received national attention in Cleveland, where he served as chairman of the platform committee and was one of the main speakers at the Townsend movement's national convention. "The Townsend plan will restore purchasing power," claimed Mahoney. "It will end unemployment. It will pay a just debt to our aged people. I shall not only vote for the Townsend Plan, but I shall fight for it until it is enacted into law." Among those sharing the platform with Mahoney were such consummate rabblerousers as Father Charles E. Coughlin (the radio priest), Gerald L.K. Smith, William Lemke, and Dr. Townsend. In this all-star lineup of Depression demagogues, Mahoney more than held his own. "He has set the convention wild with his oratory," reported the *Oregon Journal*.

By contrast, McNary kept a low profile and stayed away from the Republican National Convention in Cleveland. "Crowds upon crowds are to be encountered," McNary explained to his sister, "and I like conditions more quiet." When the Senate adjourned for the summer, McNary returned to Fir Cone. He was not looking forward to the fall campaign. "I do despise that part of political life—running for office," he wrote his sister, "but I take it about as easy as anyone can because I let the other fellow do all the talking and abusing and that usually works against a chap of that type." He characterized Mahoney as "a bad actor." McNary added, "I shall not pay much attention to his candidacy but will discuss now and then public problems."

It was one of the ironies of McNary's political career that his re-election bid was in jeopardy because of defections from senior citizens. He had always been a staunch supporter of social programs for the aging. In 1919 he had been a chief sponsor of an old-age pension bill. During the New Deal, he had worked with FDR in the development of Social Security and had supported a more comprehensive plan than the administration's final draft. One of his rare Senate speeches had been an endorsement of Social Security. Even though Roosevelt's program might not be adequate, McNary said, it represented a beginning, "The demand for decent care for our dependent aged is rooted in the fundamentals and ideals of our democracy."

Oregon Democrats were worried that Roosevelt might openly support McNary. The President had already endorsed Nebraska Republican Senator George Norris, who had been a key New Deal ally. In a 1935 visit to Oregon, Democratic National Chairman James A. Farley had praised McNary for cooperating with the administration. A year later, Congressman Pierce wrote

Farley. "You said plenty to pay the debt of gratitude we owe to the Minority Leader in your last address in Portland. I don't blame, in any way, shape, manner or form, our President's supporting Norris, he certainly deserves it. But advise him to just keep 'hands off' Oregon."

Although Roosevelt did not want to lose McNary in the Senate, he followed Pierce's advice and did not intervene in the Oregon race. With the odds favoring another FDR landslide, McNary distanced himself from Kansas Governor Alf M. Landon, the Republican presidential nominee. Richard L. Neuberger wrote that McNary had been "silent as seacoast mist on the presidential issue."

Frank Tierney, executive secretary of Oregon's Democratic Party, wrote Farley, "McNary is playing a cagey game. He absents himself from Portland and other places when [vice-presidential nominee Colonel Frank] Knox, and other out of state speakers come into Oregon." McNary declined to have the Oregon Republican State Central Committee sign his page in the *Official Voters Pamphlet*, and used his own signature as if he were an independent.

Portland Democratic leader W.A. Delzell wrote Farley that Mahoney was within striking distance of an upset. "It is a 'hoss race' and anything might happen," said Delzell. Oregon's U.S. Attorney Carl Donaugh told the national chairman that McNary "has a harder fight this year than heretofore." Donaugh predicted that the Townsend vote might tilt the election to Mahoney. Tierney wrote Farley, "Oregon voters are witnessing one of the most colorful and effective personal campaigns that any candidate has waged in Oregon for any office in a decade."

The hard-driving Mahoney never let up, making at least eight stops daily, and in a three-week period, addressing more than 50,000 people. McNary campaigned at a more leisurely pace. "We old men must retire," he declared at a GOP picnic at Fir Cone, "but I'm going to keep fighting till someone carries me out." Late in October, though, the senator suspended all campaign activities when his brother John McNary died, followed three days later, by the death of his closest Republican colleague, Senator James Couzens of Michigan. Despite his low profile in the closing days of the campaign, McNary remained a strong favorite. The *New York Times* flatly predicted another McNary landslide.

On 3 November 1936, the McNarys voted early at Chemekta School and listened to the election returns that night at Fir Cone. While McNary had anticipated an overwhelming Roosevelt victory, he was caught by surprise at the dimensions of the FDR landslide. The president was capturing forty-six of the forty-eight states. For the first time in 80 years, Pennsylvania had voted for a Democratic presidential candidate. Eight of McNary's Republican colleagues had been defeated for re-election. Three others, who had been heavily favored, Arthur Capper of Kansas, Wallace White of Maine, and Styles Bridges of New Hampshire, were clinging to hairbreadth margins.

From the earliest returns, McNary and Mahoney were locked in a virtual dead heat. The Democratic candidate had held McNary to a draw in Portland and was showing surprising strength in normally Republican rural counties. When McNary went to bed in the wee hours, the outcome was very much in doubt. By the next day, it was apparent that McNary had persevered, edging out his Democratic opponent by little more than a percentage point, a winning margin of 5,510 votes. In Multnomah County, where McNary had always rolled up huge pluralities, he led Mahoney by just a thousand votes. Mahoney had benefited from the national Democratic landslide and the Townsendite movement. McNary, as always, received a strong farm and labor vote. To his family, the senator confided his private hurt and disappointment at his close call. And yet it was no small accomplishment that McNary had survived the worst defeat in the long history of the Republican Party.

For seven years, McNary and Barkley sat across the aisle in their front-row Senate desks and conferred frequently each day on legislative matters. The Kentucky Democrat once described McNary as "the only real leader" in the Senate.

Among McNary's political proteges was Henry Cabot Lodge, Jr., of Massachusetts whose grandfather had been the Oregon senator's legislative mentor. (Author's collection)

McNary at a Washington Senators baseball game (top) with two powerful Texas Democrats, House Majority Leader Rayburn and Vice President Garner, both McNary intimates.

In the summer of 1937, McNary (bottom) engineered FDR's defeat on the "court-packing" bill. (Both author's collection)

Senator Burton K. Wheeler (top), a liberal Democrat from Montana, provided the rhetoric and McNary plotted the strategy for the bipartisan coalition that blocked FDR's plan to reorganize the Supreme Court.

During the 1937 Supreme Court reorganization fight, McNary (inset) advised the opposition that restraint would prevail. It did. (Both author's collection)

17

"Let Them Do the Talking"

IN THE AFTERMATH of FDR's 1936 landslide, the Republican minority in the Senate was reduced to sixteen. Noting his party's declining political fortunes, McNary wryly commented that he would be lucky to get tickets for Roosevelt's second inaugural. Political writers who should have known better eulogized the Republican Party. Roosevelt's advisers were hopeful that the Democratic party could be remolded into a new liberal majority.

With overwhelming majorities in both houses of Congress, FDR was confident that he could now get anything he wanted. On 5 February 1937, he dropped a bombshell. Angered by the Supreme Court's invalidation of the National Recovery Act and the Agriculture Adjustment Act, the president announced that he would submit legislation that would enlarge the court from nine to fifteen members. Roosevelt asserted that the court was dominated by tired old men who could not keep up with the workload, which was far from the truth. The Supreme Court's four reactionaries—Pierce Butler, James McReynolds, George Sutherland, and Willis Van Devanter—were opposed to the New Deal from the start. Three distinguished liberal justices, Harlan Fiske Stone, Louis Brandeis, and Benjamin Cardozo, viewed FDR's social reforms favorably. And the court's moderates, Chief Justice Charles Evans Hughes and Owen Roberts, cast the decisive votes nullifying key New Deal measures. Roosevelt's ambush on the high court was one of the most fateful decisions of his presidency, and it touched off the longest and most divisive political struggle of the New Deal. In challenging the court, FDR was seeking to defeat a national symbol and cherished ideal. Most Americans supported Roosevelt's programs that had been nullified by the court, yet they did not want him to tamper with the sanctity of the judicial branch of government. After the court's rejection of the National Recovery Act, McNary said that Congress should draft the same legislation within the defined limits of the constitution. The Oregon senator said that a constitutional amendment might be the necessary approach, but in the meantime he said that the administration should keep the NRA running through agreements between industry and labor. Roosevelt said that the NRA decision showed that the court was a throwback to the "horse and buggy" era. When the court struck down the AAA, McNary was disappointed but instead of denouncing the decision, he said it meant that the farm bloc should work with the administration in developing a new program for agriculture. So while the Oregon senator had shared FDR's frustration in the court's actions, he felt that the president's scheme was an attempt to undercut the constitutional separation of powers.

Most political observers expected FDR to win his court-packing fight. But McNary thought otherwise. Shortly after Roosevelt unveiled his court plan, the Senate minority leader polled his Republican colleagues and found them united in their opposition. Even Senator Norris, a New Deal loyalist, was against FDR's proposal. So was Johnson of California, who had twice endorsed Roosevelt. "I will try to prevent the President's sinister grasp of power," Senator Johnson wrote his son. "I fear that in the next few years, we'll be very close to a dictatorship. The congress, of course, is worse than subservient, and no one man can prevent what is happening, but at least an official as old as I am, with little in the future for him, can stand on his feet and make clear the situation." Senators Borah and Vandenberg, the GOP's two most eloquent orators, were ready to lead the charge. McNary asked them to hold back. The Senate Minority Leader told the two senators that the Democrats would be sharply divided and were already grumbling about FDR's court plan. McNary outlined his strategy for effective opposition, making the argument that if the GOP kept in the background, the Democrats would soon be attacking Roosevelt and fighting each other. "Let them do the talking," said McNary. "We'll do the voting."

Borah and Vandenberg bought McNary's strategy and the other Senate Republicans fell into line. McNary also asked national party leaders to keep silent so that FDR could not make his court plan a partisan issue that might make it more difficult for Democrats to join the opposition. Governor Alf M. Landon, the 1936 Republican presidential nominee, and GOP National Chairman John D.M. Hamilton were persuaded to show restraint.

Herbert Hoover was another matter. McNary thought the former president might blow the whole act. Hoover had already blasted the court plan and was set to give a major speech on the issue over a national radio hookup. In an effort to head him off, McNary conferred with Borah and Vandenberg. Since McNary and Borah knew that Hoover disliked them, the senators asked Vandenberg to make the approach. With some trepidation, the Michigan senator phoned Hoover and explained the Republican strategy on the court bill. Before making any commitment, Hoover demanded to know who wanted him quiet. On learning that it was McNary and Borah, the former president exploded, ripping both of the western progressives, and vowing that he would have nothing to do with either of them. Vandenberg, however, managed to convince the former president that McNary offered the best chance of protecting the Supreme Court from Roosevelt's power play.

For the next five months, McNary's strategy worked. Senator Burton K. Wheeler of Montana, a Democratic progressive who had been one of Roosevelt's most dependable allies, came out against the court bill. In March, Wheeler showed the Senate Judiciary Committee a letter from Chief Justice Hughes which demonstrated that Roosevelt was wrong in charging that the court had not kept up with its workload. Since Roosevelt would not publicly admit that his real goal was a progressive majority on the court, the Hughes letter effectively repudiated FDR's stated raison d'etre for the court bill. Hughes, who did not address the merits of FDR's proposal, was determined to block it. In the spring, Hughes and Roberts voted with the court's liberals in upholding the Wagner Labor Relations Act, the Social Security Act, the Farm Mortgage Moratorium Act, and a minimum wage law. These votes weakened Roosevelt's claim that a restructuring of the court was urgently needed and gave other Democrats the excuse they were looking for to vote against the court bill. Senators Wheeler and Borah persuaded Justice Van

Devanter that his resignation would be another major blow to FDR's forces. When the aging justice announced that he was stepping down, McNary urged the president to shelve his proposal to expand the court. Roosevelt, though, was still going for it all, and losing Democratic support.

Drew Pearson and Robert S. Allen reported that the Democratic insurgents were relying heavily on McNary's counsel. "McNary not once has appeared in the forefront," they wrote, "yet behind the scenes he has been the mastermind of the fight against the president. The antis never have made a major move without consulting him. Senator Wheeler, their titular generalissimo, holds on to McNary's coattails like a child to its mother's apron-string."

On 18 May 1937, the Senate Judiciary Committee reported unfavorably on FDR's proposal. Roosevelt then began moving toward a compromise that would have permitted the appointment of two or three new justices instead of a half dozen. The president told Senate Majority Leader Joseph Robinson that he could have the Van Devanter seat if the Senate approved legislation enlarging the court's membership. McNary, who knew that Robinson had long wanted an appointment to the Supreme Court, urged his immediate nomination and promised swift confirmation by the Senate. But Roosevelt would not formally submit Robinson's name until the majority leader delivered other new vacancies for the White House to fill.

With characteristic determination, Robinson set out to find the votes for a compromise that would permit FDR to expand the high court by one justice a year. Day and night, the sixty-five-year-old Robinson cajoled his colleagues to help him achieve his lifetime ambition. On 14 July, Robinson died of a heart attack while reading the *Congressional Record* in his apartment. McNary and many of Robinson's colleagues blamed his death on the stress caused by the court fight.

"I feel particularly depressed because of our close association for the twenty years I have been in the Senate," McNary wrote his brother-in-law. "He died a martyr to the cause of the court plan which never should have been presented to a civilized legislative organization." McNary wrote Mrs. Robinson, "No one outside of yourself and family could feel more depressed and saddened than I do about the passing of your beloved husband. For years we have been close and intimate friends and our relationship was as close as that of two brothers."

Without Robinson, the president could not come close to winning a showdown vote on the court. Vice President Garner bluntly told FDR, "You are beat. You haven't got the votes." McNary conceived the motion that finally killed Roosevelt's plan, a simple move to recommit the bill to the hostile Judiciary Committee. Just a week after Robinson's death, the Senate sent the measure back to the committee by a vote of seventy to twenty.

McNary's prestige had been vastly enhanced by the court fight. The informal coalition of Republicans and conservative Democrats that he helped forge in opposition to FDR on this issue would remain the dominant voting bloc in the Senate for nearly a generation. When Vandenberg attempted to formalize the new coalition with a "Conservative Manifesto," McNary shot him down. The Oregon senator had a better understanding of party politics than Vandenberg, and he knew that institutionalizing the coalition would be a tactical blunder. Before the Michigan senator had a chance to go public with his manifesto, McNary had leaked it to reporters, and Vandenberg became entwined in too much controversy to get support for his resolution.

The split among Senate Democrats was further exacerbated by FDR's intervention in the contest to succeed Robinson as majority leader. Senator Pat Harrison of Mississippi, the witty, politically astute chairman of the Finance Committee, had been Robinson's chief lieutenant and was McNary's closest friend in the Senate. While Harrison was a conservative, he was a party loyalist and had been the driving force behind the passage of Social Security, the National Recovery Act, and other important New Deal measures. Harrison had, however, clashed with FDR on a tax bill, and the president had not forgotten about it. The White House threw its support to Senator Alben Barkley of Kentucky, the affable, kindly, liberal assistant leader, who, in FDR's judgment, would be easier to control. Barkley edged Harrison by a single vote. Although FDR considered this an important victory, it strained his relations with the senate, for even his allies resented his interference in legislative matters.

McNary's relationship with Barkley was less intimate than his friendship with Joe Robinson had been, yet they worked well together. The Oregon Senator liked Barkley's rich humor and homespun country stories. Barkley was somewhat in awe of his Republican counterpart, describing McNary as "a legislative genius." On one occasion when a Democratic senator asked

Barkley how to vote, the Senate majority leader threw up his hands and said, "I don't know. Ask Charley McNary. He's the only real leader around here."

What gave McNary an advantage over Barkley was his mastery of parliamentary rules and procedures. The minority leader joked that outmaneuvering the genial Barkley was "as enjoyable as golf and considerably less expensive." McNary classified legislation into three categories which he nicknamed "demagoguers," "poisoners," and "hot potatoes." The first category included such popular issues as old-age pensions or increased veterans benefits that Republicans would introduce and force the majority Democrats to take responsibility for defeating the measure or come up with the money. In one such instance, McNary's young protege, Henry Cabot Lodge, offered an amendment that would have raised pensions for the elderly by a third. When Lodge's amendment was rejected it put the Democrats in the position of opposing senior citizens. The court bill fit McNary's definition of a "poisoner" in which the Republicans kept silent and watched the controversial legislation spread its poison among the Democrats. The "hot potatoes" required senators of McNary's own party to make difficult and sometimes unpopular choices, as in cutting appropriations for social welfare programs. In the wake of the court fight, McNary noted that the Senate really had three political parties—Democrats, Republicans, and New Dealers. In 1937 and again in 1938, McNary helped block Roosevelt's attempt to reorganize the executive branch by implementing his poisoner strategy. In 1939, he worked offstage with conservative Democratic leaders and by one vote slashed $150 million from FDR's budget.

McNary's tight connections with the Senate's real Democratic power structure helped make these victories possible. The uncrowned leader of this power elite was Vice President Garner. The craggy-faced, cigar-smoking "Cactus Jack" had formerly been speaker of the U.S. House of Representatives and was a matchless wheeler dealer. Never an insider with Roosevelt, Garner broke with the president after the court struggle and worked with the emerging Senate coalition. McNary and Harrison often drank bonded bourbon with Garner and plotted political strategy in the vice president's office just off the Senate chamber. The three men were avid baseball fans and often continued their discussions in a front-row box at Griffith Stadium when the Washington Senators baseball club was in town.

On the Senate floor, McNary rarely gave a speech and he was unimpressed with grandiloquent oratory and florid gestures. Watching Vandenberg rehearsing a speech, the Oregon senator told him, "That's fine, Van, only don't deliver it again." McNary bristled at meetings when Borah would get pontifical. "I hate a man who demogogues when the doors are closed," snorted McNary. Even so, he admitted that it was sometimes difficult to maintain his cool demeanor in Senate debate. "When I thought I couldn't stand it any longer," said McNary, "I used to pinch my leg. I would keep on pinching until the impulse was over. After a good many debates in the past few years, I would get home and find I'd pinched myself black and blue."

McNary's unofficial whip and political lieutenant was Henry Cabot Lodge, Jr., of Massachusetts, the grandson and namesake of the Oregon senator's old mentor. Tall, athletic, with chiseled good looks, Lodge was thirty-four years old when he was elected to the Senate in 1936 over James Michael Curley, the legendary Democratic political boss who was the prototype for Frank Skeffington in Edwin O'Connor's *The Last Hurrah*. Just as the elder Lodge had taken McNary in hand, the Oregon Republican took the younger Lodge as his protege. Lodge quickly learned the techniques of procedural manipulation and McNary often designated him to watch the floor. Joseph Alsop and Robert Kitner reported that Lodge caused the Democrats more trouble in the 1937 session than any other senator. FDR accused young Lodge of being too political, but McNary viewed him as a young man of great promise. "My most cherished recollection of service in the Senate was my friendship with Senator McNary," Lodge recalled years later. "He was very much like a father to me."

In 1938 McNary had much more to say about national party strategy in the midterm elections than had been the case four years earlier when Hoover's forces still controlled the GOP national committee. Working with Landon and Hamilton, McNary thwarted Hoover's attempt to schedule a midterm Republican National Convention. McNary and Landon successfully argued that such a gathering would be divisive at a time when the party should be displaying a united front.

Heading into the 1938 elections, the Democrats were anything but united. Embittered over his setback in the court fight, Roosevelt tried to purge three conservative Democratic senators in the primaries—Walter George of Georgia, Millard Tydings of

Maryland, and "Cotton Ed" Smith of South Carolina. But in each instance, FDR struck out, and his efforts alienated him still further from Democratic conservatives. In McNary's home state, the Roosevelt Administration helped block the renomination of Democratic Governor Charles H. Martin, a feisty retired general who had been critical of the New Deal. Former Oregon Governor Oswald West wrote James A. Farley after Martin's defeat that the purging of the governor had undone the work of more than a decade in rebuilding the state's Democratic party.

McNary told Republicans that the divisions within the Democratic party and the faltering economy gave them an opportunity for strong gains in the November elections. "We have got to present a progressive front and deal generously with the farmer, deal fairly with organized labor, advocate additional social security, and treat business fairly," said McNary. Above all, the Senate minority leader said that the GOP "could not go back to its old reactionaryism."

The GOP made its strongest showing in a decade in the 1938 midterm elections, picking up eight seats in the Senate, eighty-one in the House of Representatives and thirteen governorships. Among the Republican winners were such bright new prospects as Senator Robert A. Taft of Ohio, and Governors Harold Stassen of Minnesota, Charles A. Sprague of Oregon, and John Bricker of Ohio. Another emerging young star was New York prosecutor Thomas E. Dewey who had come within a hair's breadth of defeating popular New York Governor Herbert Lehman.

"As everybody with any sense knew it would," stated the *Christian Science Monitor*, "the Republican party has revived."

For his role in the party's comeback, Charles L. McNary was once again a name to be reckoned with in presidential politics.

When Medford lawyer
Alfred E. Reames was
sworn in as Oregon's jun-
ior U.S. Senator by Vice
President John Nance Gar-
ner in 1938, McNary
congratulated his Demo-
cratic colleague (top).
Reames had been ap-
pointed by Governor
Charles Martin to serve the
remainder of Senator
Frederick Steiwer's term
following his resignation.

McNary caricatured
(bottom) in a 1938 *Philadelphia Record* as riding the
GOP elephant. (Both au-
thor's collection)

While McNary never liked top hats, he donned one for the 1939 dedication of the Thomas Jefferson Memorial on the capital's Tidal Basin. He had been among the chief planners of the monument to one of his political heroes. The senator was accompanied by Cornelia and their daughter Charlotte. (Both author's collection)

18

Seeking the Top

ON 26 OCTOBER 1939, Charles Linza McNary announced that he was a candidate for president of the United States. While the Senate minority leader said that he would not actively seek the Republican presidential nomination, he told reporters that he would permit supporters in western states to place his name before the 1940 GOP national convention. "In no sense am I interested," he said, "except for the purpose of getting together on some other candidate."

Few politicians took McNary's public disclaimer at face value. If he could capture the presidential nomination, the Oregon Republican very much wanted it. His hopes were pegged to a deadlocked convention in which he might emerge as the unifying compromise candidate. McNary planned to avoid the primaries and by remaining on the sidelines, he felt it would strengthen his position as everybody's second choice. Senator Vandenberg was seeded as the early front-runner with Taft and Dewey on his heels. Hoover had launched a comeback, and several political columnists were promoting a handsome businessman named Wendell L. Willkie as a possible dark horse entry.

One of the reasons that McNary changed his mind about running for the presidency after passing up much more glittering opportunities in 1928 and 1936 was that he realized 1940 would be his last chance. McNary would be sixty-six years old in June, and he was already the oldest man in the field, two months older than the former president. The Oregon Republican had been encouraged to run by some of the most influential western progressives—Borah of Idaho, Capper of Kansas, and Nye of North Dakota. Landon made it known that McNary was his kind of candidate. For months, Governor Sprague of Oregon had been pressing McNary to get into the presidential race. By the fall of 1939, McNary gave his friends the answer they had wanted to hear.

His campaign team was headed by Sprague, Portland lawyer and mortgage banker Ralph H. Cake, and Palmer Hoyt, publisher of the *Oregonian*. McNary designated Oregon GOP chairman Kern Crandall as his campaign's official spokesman. In late December of 1939, Cake wrote Senator McNary: "I am still convinced that there is opening up a wonderful opportunity for your candidacy, but that it should not be an open and avowed candidacy at this time. Also, I still feel that your effort should be confined, so far as the public is concerned, entirely to the State of Oregon. I know that behind the scenes you are laying the groundwork for the opportunity to step in when these avowed candidates have deadlocked themselves."

Even after announcing his candidacy, McNary sought to act as if he was above the battle. When the National Press Club invited him to share a platform with the other GOP contenders, McNary declined. Responding to General Hugh S. Johnson's column about his presidential chances in 1940, McNary wrote Johnson: "A substantial part of my legislative activities have been engaged in removing surpluses, not adding to them."

In a 25 January 1940 letter to Crandall, McNary outlined his assessment of their campaign. "I am not an active candidate, and if I were, it would react to our disadvantage. That is my opinion. I know the great outlay necessary to promote an active candidacy, the tremendous outlay necessary to promote an aggressive candidacy. We have not such resources, nor would I want them employed in that direction if we did. In my opinion our prospects are brighter under an unobtrusive program. All the candidates are friendly, and really it is only by last will and testament that we can assume the state of heirship. At all times I am conscious of the many hurdles that lie between."

With the exception of his home state, McNary was staying out of the primaries, where he hoped the other candidates might get knocked from contention. In Wisconsin, Dewey ended Vandenberg's reign as the front-runner, winning more than 60 percent of the vote and sweeping the entire slate of delegates. *Life* magazine called Dewey the "Number One Glamour Boy of the G.O.P." and the Gallup poll reported that he was the favorite of nearly half of all Republican voters.

"He is a personable fellow, dynamic, and belongs to that group sometimes referred to as pep talkers," McNary wrote his sister about Dewey. "Mr. Dewey has plenty of arms, ammunition and implements of war to carry him through and that is required if one is in dead earnest to win the nomination."

In the Nebraska primary, McNary tried to slow the Dewey bandwagon by endorsing Vandenberg as a better friend of the farmers than the New Yorker. Dewey, however, scored another impressive victory and eliminated Vandenberg as a major candidate. In Maryland and New Jersey, Senator Taft pulled out to avoid the humiliation of getting wiped out by Dewey. Taft concentrated his effort in the boss-controlled caucus states and remained close to Dewey in the overall delegate count. "It appears to me," Cake told McNary in late April, "that the fight is becoming so strong between Taft and Dewey that they cannot possibly be nominated themselves."

When an *Oregonian* poll taken in February reported that Dewey held an edge over McNary in Portland, some McNary men were concerned about the senator's ability to hold his own state. But Dewey, who had been deferential to the Senate minority leader, recognized that it would be considered bad form to campaign against him in Oregon. On 17 May 1940, McNary easily won the Oregon primary, receiving 133,488 votes to Dewey's 5,190. It was the only time that Oregon voters had endorsed a favorite son in their presidential primary and the overwhelming vote assured him the unanimous support of Oregon's delegation to the Republican National Convention. "I accept the compliment and appreciate the confidence and esteem in which I am held by the people of my native state," he wrote his sister, "but that is all there is to it."

McNary's backers maintained that he represented the party's best hope of regaining the critical farm and labor vote. In the spring, *Time* magazine suggested that the nomination of McNary by the GOP convention "would automatically attract otherwise safely Democratic votes." The weekly newsmagazine reported that such party heavyweights as Landon, House Minority Leader Joseph Martin, and New York Republican national committeeman Kenneth Simpson were all pushing McNary as a compromise candidate. "Their most audacious dream" according to

Time, was a ticket of McNary for president and the fiery and colorful New York mayor, Fiorello LaGuardia for vice president. Such a combination, *Time* said, "would convince: 1) Franklin Roosevelt that he is too tired to run again; 2) the U.S. that the GOP is sincerely progressive; and 3) the farm and labor vote that they should go Republican."

Kyle Palmer, the political editor of the *Los Angeles Times* and an important power broker in the California Republican party, wrote in April that McNary might well be the chief beneficiary of the primary wars between the other contenders. Palmer said that McNary "has a vote appeal with which many party leaders throughout the country are becoming more and more interested. Because of his long service in Washington, his lifelong liberalism, McNary unquestionably would have much to recommend him to the electorate, regardless of partisan affiliations. His intimate association with most of the major issues that have come before Congress since 1920 has made him known to the country generally, and from a geographical standpoint he is regarded as especially well situated."

McNary contended that the Republicans should look westward in the 1940 presidential election because it was doubtful that anyone could defeat FDR in the northeastern industrial states, which were becoming increasingly Democratic. "The East will not be the battleground in 1940 for the party," asserted the Oregon senator. "The Republican party can win if it satisfies the West that it intends to place agriculture on equality with industry."

On the Democratic side, FDR had not made known his intentions, yet his actions seemed to indicate that he would seek a third term. Although McNary believed in the two-term tradition, he discouraged Senate colleagues from introducing a resolution against a third term, telling them that such a proposal would be "ill-advised and ill-mannered." When every politician in the land was trying to determine whether or not Roosevelt was running, a top presidential aide told Richard L. Neuberger that McNary was among the few who knew FDR's plans. "If Charley McNary doesn't know whether the President is going to run again, I don't know who does," said James H. Rowe. "McNary probably sees the President oftener than anyone in Washington outside his own immediate family."

Roosevelt confided to Harold Ickes that because of the World War he was thinking about proposing a bipartisan unity ticket with McNary replacing John Nance Garner as his running-mate. Ickes told FDR that the addition of McNary "undoubtedly would make an unusually strong ticket." FDR, however, knew that McNary would be dubious of such an unusual move.

The president's trial balloon for a unity ticket may have been his invitation to McNary and two other Republican leaders to attend the annual Democratic Jackson Day dinner. "I sincerely appreciate this cordial and courteous invitation," replied McNary, "but I shall be unable to attend."

Roosevelt opened his dinner remarks by teasing his old friend. "Once upon a time," said FDR, "there was a school teacher, who, after describing Heaven in alluring and golden terms, asked her class of small boys how many of them wanted to go to Heaven. With eyes that sparkled at the thought every small boy in the class held up his hand—except one. Teacher said, 'Why Charles, Charley McNary, Charley you don't want to go to Heaven? Why not?' 'Teacher,' he said, 'sure I want to go to Heaven, but pointing to the rest of the boys in the room, 'not with that bunch.'" The president's story brought the house down, and McNary chortled when he read about it the next morning.

In seeking the GOP nomination, McNary stepped up his criticism of FDR. On a national radio broadcast, the Senate minority leader spoke of the New Deal's waste and inefficiency and described the Republicans as "the party of hope" who would "provide more jobs for workers in factories, larger incomes on farms and security for the unemployed."

Although the Republican race had tightened, McNary simply had not done enough in his own behalf to take advantage of the moment. As Senate Minority Leader, he was pursuing the presidential nomination with a classic insiders strategy, relying on his reputation in Washington, and the help of his Senate colleagues.

In many ways, McNary's 1940 campaign was the forerunner of the losing presidential bids of Senate Majority Leader Lyndon B. Johnson in 1960 and Senate Republican Leader Howard H. Baker in 1980. Each of the three men overestimated the importance of their Senate leadership positions and failed to make an all-out effort to win their party's nominations.

William Allen White, publisher of the Emporia *Daily Gazette*, and a Kansas delegate to the 1940 GOP national convention, told Oregon journalist Richard L. Neuberger that McNary would make an admirable president, but said his chances were slim. "It just seems out of the realm of possibility so fine a man as McNary should be a Republican nominee," wrote White. Neuberger, who had made a profitable free-lance career writing about the politicians of the Pacific Northwest, was undaunted and wrote a pre-convention McNary profile for *Life* that portrayed the Oregon Senator as "the one GOP candidate capable of clinching the rural vote and victory." Neuberger wrote McNary, "If the Republican convention is deadlocked, you might possibly emerge as the nominee."

On the eve of the convention, the European war suddenly overshadowed all domestic issues and normal political considerations. Hitler's armies that had already swallowed Denmark, Norway, Belgium and Poland had overrun France, and the lights of democracy were flickering throughout Europe. "My situation is no nearer settled," McNary wrote his sister on 17 June. "It may be a lot more uncertain because this morning's extra papers announce that France has quit. I do not know what effect this will have on the public mind or on the administration."

After the fall of France, McNary knew that he had probably been eliminated as a serious contender for the presidential nomination. The Oregon senator had underestimated the threat of Nazi Germany, and his record of isolationism in the Thirties did not exactly inspire confidence in a time of world crisis. McNary was not the only GOP hopeful whose political fortunes dropped because of the sudden turn of events on the battlefields of Western Europe. Dewey's youth and his isolationist rhetoric became overnight liabilities and his lead over the Republican pack was narrowing. Taft and Hoover were making their moves to overtake him, but they had been equally wrong about the war. Willkie, who had been dismissed as a long shot only a few days earlier, was coming on strong because he had been warning the nation for months about the danger of Hitler. Indeed, the plain-spoken Hoosier had been straightforward in saying that Americans might have to go to war in order to defeat fascism. His face was suddenly splashed across the front of a half dozen national magazines and the Gallup poll reported that his popularity had surged. Although Willkie had few pledged delegates, he was the only candidate who was conveying a sense of movement and excitement.

As the convention opened, FDR caught the Republican delegates by surprise when he named two of the GOP's most respected interventionists, Henry L. Stimson, and Colonel Frank Knox, the 1936 vice-presidential nominee, to join the cabinet as secretary of war and secretary of the navy.

For the first time in his long career, McNary decided to attend his party's national convention. Wearing a white suit, the Oregon senator took the train to Philadelphia and checked into the Bellevue-Stratford, the old hotel on South Broad Street which was serving as the convention's official headquarters. In the lobby of the hotel, McNary denounced Willkie as "a tool of Wall Street" and predicted that he would get no more than 250 votes. "The West, which the Republican party must carry, will go against us if Mr. Willkie heads the ticket," McNary declared. Ralph Cake, who was managing McNary's campaign in Philadelphia, looked stricken. Cake thought that the senator's words were counterproductive and made Willkie seem all the more viable. McNary, however, was determined to try to stop Willkie and joined other isolationist senators and congressmen in urging the convention to reject the interventionist Willkie.

McNary did not like what he was seeing in Philadelphia. "This game is only for millionaires or those that have their support," he wrote his sister on Bellevue stationary. "Tree growers better stay at home. Have seen the Oregon delegation and that brought me here. I never did like the people and town. Streets are narrow and buildings covered with soot."

Though McNary's idea of a deadlocked convention was about to become reality, he had no illusions about his chances. "I told a number of delegates not to waste any votes on me," he wrote his wife. "I shall be glad when it is all settled. When I left yesterday I thought the drift was toward Mr. Taft. He would make an excellent president." Returning to Washington, McNary wrote his sister, "Philadelphia is a mess and I was glad to get away. They are telephoning me to return, but I told them to be calm, think it over and telephone me later this afternoon. I am trying to keep away as far as I can from this political conflict."

On Thursday night, McNary was nominated for the presidency by former Oregon congressman W.A. Ekwall, who described him as "a man who can unquestionably win in November and who, measured from every conceivable standpoint, has the stature, the bearing and the ability to become a great president of this nation." Before the first ballot got underway, nine other men were placed in nomination. Already the crowds in the galleries were shouting their "We Want Willkie" chant.

As expected, Dewey led the first roll call with 360 votes, followed by Taft with 189, Willkie with 105, and Vandenberg with 76. McNary trailed far behind the leaders with 13 votes. After the first ballot, Dewey began slipping, while Taft and Willkie steadily gained. On the fourth ballot, Willkie moved into the lead.

Soon afterward, Cake arranged a meeting with Alf M. Landon, who was chairman of the Kansas delegation, and House minority leader Joseph Martin, the convention chairman who controlled most of the Massachusetts delegation. Cake said that both Landon and Martin decided to release their delegates to Taft in a final effort to block Willkie. But, on the next ballot, it was Willkie rather than Taft who picked up the lion's share of delegates from the two swing states. Cake immediately telephoned McNary. "Ralph, go back to the Oregon delegation," instructed the senator, "and tell them to vote for Mr. Willkie. He's going to be nominated."

Shortly after midnight, Oregon's votes switched to Willkie amid the "We Want Willkie" frenzy of the galleries, and the outsider went over the top to win the 1940 Republican presidential nomination. Ralph Cake then went to work in trying to get McNary the second spot on the ticket.

McNary and New York Congressman Sol Bloom, chairman of the House Foreign Affairs Committee, escorted King George VI and Queen Elizabeth of England into the Capitol during their 1939 state visit. Bloom and McNary stand at the Queen's left. (Author's collection)

At a 1938 meeting of the Republican National Committee, McNary conferred with (clockwise) party chairman John D. M. Hamilton, Mrs. Worthington Scranton of Pennsylvania, and Arthur Vandenberg of Michigan. (Author's collection)

19

"A Damn Totem Pole"

THERE WERE ONLY two problems with Ralph Cake's scheme to get McNary second billing on the Republican ticket. The Oregon senator did not want it. And, even if McNary were to have a change of heart, Willkie had already promised the job to someone else.

McNary dismissed the vice presidency as "a damn totem pole." His disdainful view of the nation's second-highest office was hardly unique. McNary's colleagues Hiram Johnson and William E. Borah had rejected GOP vice-presidential nominations in 1920 and 1924. John Nance Garner, who bitterly regretted his decision to step down as House speaker to become FDR's vice president, asserted that the position "isn't worth a warm pitcher of spit." Humorist Will Rogers had told the story about the two brothers: one ran off to sea, the other became vice president, and neither was ever heard from again. "It isn't a crime exactly. Ye can't be sint to jail f'r it," cracked Mr. Dooley, "but it's a kind iv a disgrace. It's like writin' anonymous letters." Although by 1940 there had been a half dozen vice presidents who inherited the White House on the death of a president, only two of these men had gone on to win a full term on their own. For most of the nation's vice presidents, the office had been a political dead end. Like Johnson and Borah, McNary genuinely preferred the Senate over the vice presidency.

Another reason for McNary's reluctance to even discuss such a possibility was that he regarded Willkie as a front man for

Wall Street financial interests. "When I saw McNary, he was bulging with rage at Willkie's nomination," recalled Joseph Alsop, "and he told me that he'd never run with him." McNary told an assistant Interior secretary, "That is one thing they cannot hand me." While McNary was in Philadelphia, Robert S. Allen asked him about the rumors that he might take second place on a Willkie ticket. "Can you imagine a public power man running on a ticket with the head of Commonwealth and Southern?" chortled McNary. "It just doesn't make sense."

But Ralph Cake thought it made a good deal of sense. McNary's reputation as a champion of public power could help offset Willkie's negative image as a private utility mogul, Cake argued. McNary's selection would also balance the ticket in other ways. Where Willkie was a political amateur, McNary was the consummate professional. At forty-eight, Willkie was FDR's junior by a full decade and relatively young for a presidential nominee. So Willkie needed an older man of national stature, and McNary, who had just turned sixty-six offered the right chronological balance. Although Willkie still claimed his native Indiana as his home state, he had lived on New York's Fifth Avenue and worked in the vicinity of Wall Street so long that he was widely regarded as a New Yorker. Cake pointed out that McNary, as a westerner, came from the right part of the country to provide geographical balance.

Moments after Willkie's nomination, Cake was turned away when he attempted to make his selling points in the candidate's suite. "The Willkie people remembered what McNary had said about their candidate," Cake recalled in 1971, "and I was told that there was no use trying to get in. They weren't going to let any McNary supporters get in to see him." Through a mutual friend, Cake reached a former Willkie business associate and got the same response. "Definitely not McNary," the man told Cake. "We remember his Wall Street statement."

In the small hours of Friday morning, Cake sought the advice of Alf M. Landon, who had long been friendly toward McNary. Cake had been active in Landon's 1936 campaign and was a former national president of Landon's college fraternity, Phi Gamma Delta. "I went over to his suite, woke him up, and told him what the situation was," Cake said later. Landon did not have to be sold on the Oregon senator. "McNary would be a good choice," he said. "Wendell Willkie, however, is the only per-

184

son who can help you." Landon told Cake that Willkie had left the Ben Franklin and was staying in an apartment at the Warwick. He then gave Cake Willkie's unlisted telephone number.

It was nearly 5 A.M. and Cake telephoned Philip Parrish, editorial page editor of the *Oregonian*, who was also campaigning for McNary, and told him that he wondered if it would be too pushy to awaken Willkie. "Mostly because we'd never been to a national convention before," recalled Cake, "I called."

When Edith Willkie answered the phone, she curtly informed Cake that her husband had been in bed for less than a half hour. "I wouldn't be calling at this hour," said Cake, "If it weren't important."

Willkie then picked up the phone and invited Cake over to his apartment. It took Cake only a few minutes to rush down the block from his hotel. "I wouldn't blame you if you kicked me out," Cake told Willkie. "I came here to talk about Senator McNary."

Wearing a blue silk bathrobe, the bearlike Willkie grinned and nodded his head. "I assumed that you were here to talk about a running mate," he said. "I'm personally in favor of Governor [Raymond] Baldwin of Connecticut. But they tell me he's too close to New York. My advisers are coming to the hotel at 10 A.M. to discuss the running mate. I suggest you shower, shave, and come over. I'll see that they have you come in. If they are willing to select Senator McNary, I'll take him."

Within an hour, McNary was getting telephone calls in Washington from party leaders and political reporters about the vice presidency. "This is Friday morning," the Oregon senator wrote his sister, "and I have been awake most of the night answering telephone calls from Philadelphia and stating over and over that I did not want to be nominated for vice president. I have given it out to the news boys to be published in the press and I hope that settles it."

McNary's persistence did not diminish Cake's enthusiasm. By the time Willkie's advisers had convened, McNary had picked up the support of three influential friends of the presidential nominee—publishers Helen Rogers Reid of the *New York Herald Tribune*, Gardner Cowles of *Look* magazine, and Roy Howard of Scripps-Howard newspapers. Among the others attending the meeting in Willkie's apartment were House Minority Leader Joseph Martin, *Time-Life* publisher Henry Luce, Governor Stassen of Minnesota, newspaper publisher John S. Knight, Connecticut GOP national committeeman Samuel Pryor, Indiana Congressman Charles Halleck, Willkie strategist Russell Davenport, and New York GOP leader Kenneth Simpson.

For more than two hours, Willkie's exhausted advisers discussed a range of possible candidates. While Taft and Dewey were quickly eliminated because of their repeated disavowals of interest, McNary's rejection was not accepted as final. Reid, Cowles, and Howard noted that the Far West had been the region most opposed to Willkie during the presidential balloting and that McNary was the region's most popular political figure. Senator Vandenberg and governors John Bricker of Ohio and Ralph Carr of Colorado were the only others who were seriously considered. While Pryor reminded the group of Willkie's commitment to Baldwin, the group's consensus was that the Connecticut governor brought little to the ticket. Vanderberg had turned down Landon's offer of the vice presidential nomination in 1936, and had done poorly in the 1940 primaries. So he, too, was scratched from the list.

Joe Martin told Willkie that McNary was the only potential running mate who would strengthen the ticket. "You are known as a utilities man," said Martin. "McNary has sided with the public power boys. You're supposed to represent big-business interests. McNary was the sponsor of the McNary-Haugen farm bill. You aren't supposed to know much about the legislative process. McNary is a master of it. I think you'd make a perfect team."

With the group converging on the Oregon senator, Willkie suggested that Martin call McNary and offer him the nomination. Cowles said years later that Willkie settled on McNary in the hope that his selection might neutralize the public power issue. Once Willkie had been persuaded to go with McNary, it still seemed doubtful that the senator would accept. "Hell no, I wouldn't run with Willkie," McNary growled when Martin made the offer. Cake then took the phone and urged him to accept because it would be the first time since the Civil War that an Oregonian had been nominated for the vice presidency by a major political party. "It's a rare opportunity for Oregon to be recognized and honored," said Cake. "You've been in your present position as a result of the people of Oregon."

McNary was softening. After a long pause, he told Cake to

put Martin back on the phone. "You have got to consider the Republican party," implored Martin. "You are in a position to do the party a great service. Your presence on the ticket would give it great strength. We'd have a better chance to win."

At this point, the Oregon senator agreed to accept the nomination if the convention chose him. "I've told them all along that I don't want the job," McNary told reporters in the Capitol barber shop. "I recognize, though, that there are some things you have to do for the sake of party. If the demand is in the nature of a draft, I will be a good soldier and do my part." In a letter to his wife, McNary added, "I was innocent of the job until yesterday morning. Then, pressure was turned on, and I finally yielded because of the implorations of the Oregon delegation who loyally supported me and who wanted the old state recognized. We shall all have to carry part of this load, but I think it will soon end after the first wave of publicity has subsided."

Following his conversation with McNary, Cake asked Congressman Harold Knutson of Minnesota to deliver the nominating speech that afternoon. Cake also lined up seven prominent Republicans to second McNary's nomination, but had to withdraw three of his invitations on learning that candidates were limited to four seconders. Senators Lodge and Vandenberg were among those who seconded McNary's nomination. Knutson told the convention that McNary was "a household word in every American farm home," while Vandenberg described the Oregonian as "the most popular legislator who ever sat in the Senate of the United States."

McNary's only opponent was Congressman Dewey Short of Missouri, a bullthroated conservative who was known as the Hamilton Fish of the Ozarks. The outcome was never in doubt. On the first ballot, McNary was nominated with 890 votes to Short's 108. At the end of the roll call, the Missouri congressman went to the podium and moved to make McNary's nomination unanimous.

The senator was dictating letters when several newspaper reporters burst into his office and told him that he had been nominated. "Well, if that's the case, let's have a smoke," said McNary as he passed around a carton of cigarettes. "I am grateful for the confidence reposed in me by the convention," he said, "but I wished they had imposed the chore on someone else."

Back home in Salem and while shopping at a grocery store, McNary's wife was stunned to learn of her husband's nomination. "I was never so surprised in my life," she said. "I didn't even know Charles was up for the vice presidency. I said it couldn't be true because Charles had wired me this morning that he wouldn't accept the nomination."

McNary wrote his sister, "I just could not avoid the responsibility. I am not happy about the situation at all. I either had to be disloyal to my friends in the party or be a soldier; and as I am a son of hardy pioneers, I had to go to battle."

His nomination received mixed reviews. "It is an unhappy choice," stated the *New York Times*, "because in many of the things that now matter most, Mr. McNary's views are the complete negation of Mr. Willkie's views." "To get the presidential and vice-presidential nominees together," declared the *New Republic*, "requires that one or the other of them throw a back somersault in the air." *Newsweek* said McNary provided strength in the areas where Willkie was most vulnerable. Richard L. Neuberger, writing in *The Nation*, called McNary the most progressive Republican on a national ticket since Teddy Roosevelt. The St. Louis *Post-Dispatch* applauded that "in choosing his running mate, Mr. Willkie, the amateur, has made a decision quite worthy of a professional." The *Boston Herald* said, "The Republicans have chosen a man possessed of far more ability than the usual candidate for the vice presidency."

Most Republican leaders were delighted that McNary had accepted. "If the party cannot win this ticket," said Senator Warren Austin of Vermont, "then it ought to be liquidated." Alf M. Landon wrote McNary, "Your name among the western delegates was greeted with great enthusiasm. The universal expression was: 'McNary sets us up at home.' I find that to be true in Kansas. I had expected it, of course, but I must say, the force and carrying power of your name on the ticket here in Kansas is even beyond my expectation."

FDR was impressed with Willkie's choice. On the morning after the GOP convention, the president referred to its nominees at a cabinet meeting. "It was the general opinion that the Republicans had nominated their strongest possible ticket," Ickes noted. "The President spoke particularly of McNary. He said that McNary had deserved the nomination and that he was glad it had gone to him, adding that he had always liked McNary, which is the fact." James A. Farley later wrote, "We all agreed that Senate Minority Leader Charles McNary added strength to the Republican ticket."

"Undoubtedly, McNary will be a strong candidate," Ickes wrote in his diary. "He has always been a champion of the farmers and he may make it hard going for us in the agricultural states. I believe that we can carry Washington and California and Montana and probably Idaho. But McNary is altogether too likely to carry Oregon for the ticket, and while he probably won't make any speeches or take any active part in the campaign, his name will have great drawing power." Ickes added, "McNary has always been a liberal Republican. He has supported many of the New Deal policies, while others he has not fought any too vigorously. He is distinctly sympathetic to public power, and for him to be running on the same ticket with a private utility magnate is sardonic, to say the least."

On the afternoon of McNary's nomination, FDR wrote him: "My very warm congratulations on your nomination for Vice President. Once upon a time—twenty years ago—I ran for Vice President. I learned a lot! I hope to see you soon." When the White House released FDR's letter to his old friend, McNary said that he was looking forward to getting some good advice on campaigning for the vice presidency.

Roosevelt had decided to run for a third term in the belief that the World War had made him indispensable in the White House. He was nominated by acclamation in Chicago in mid-July but had to exert pressure on the delegates—including a threat to withdraw—in order to get Henry A. Wallace approved as his running-mate. The secretary of agriculture had been a lifelong Republican prior to joining the Roosevelt Administration and a great many old-line Democrats were unhappy when FDR picked him for vice president. Wallace was chosen partly because his popularity in the farm belt rivaled McNary's. On the convention floor, a western delegate shouted, "Henry's our answer to Charley McNary!"

"Both the Democratic nominees are warm friends of mine," McNary wrote his wife on 19 July. "President Roosevelt told several people that if he could not make it, he would rather see me there than anyone, and Wallace has told the newspaper boys from time to time that Republicans should nominate me. That part is nice—to have no ill feelings against your opponents."

Early in July, McNary met Willkie for the first time. The presidential candidate was in the bathtub when McNary arrived at his hotel suite, and Willkie invited him into the bathroom. The senator later joked that Willkie had "a very human side to him that was charming." They conferred for more than two hours, and McNary was pleasantly surprised to find that Willkie was not a Wall Street extremist but, rather, an old-fashioned liberal. McNary advised Willkie to be more discreet in his public utterances. "Don't forget young fellow," McNary told Willkie, "in politics, you'll never get in trouble by not saying too much."

The 1940 presidential election marked the last time that the major party candidates accepted their nominations in hometown notification ceremonies rather than in the convention hall. It was a tradition that had preceded the age of Lincoln and Douglas, although FDR had broken it in 1932 with a dramatic appearance in Chicago Stadium. Willkie was returning to Elwood, Indiana in August to formally accept the presidential nomination, and McNary was scheduled to accept his nomination in Salem a week later. McNary offered to hold the ceremonies at Fir Cone, opening his farm to the public "provided they don't run over my trees." He promptly withdrew the invitation when Governor Sprague and Cake told him that a grove of filberts would have to be removed to make room for the anticipated crowds. "Not by a damn sight," McNary shot back. "I'd rather have the filbert trees than the job."

Sprague and Cake then booked the Oregon State fairgrounds. McNary was unhappy at reports that civic leaders were planning to make a big production out of the ceremony. "That is just what I don't want them to do," he wrote his sister. "I am not running for Mayor of Salem and I don't like demonstrations anyhow. It will go along as it was ordained, in a dignified way. I have about completed my acceptance speech and I believe you will all like it fairly well."

When one of Willkie's closest advisers suggested that McNary not bring up the controversial public power issue in his speech, the Oregon senator cut him short. "It's an issue in two places," replied McNary. " In my part of the country, and in my conscience." McNary reiterated his support of public ownership of water power in his text and showed an advance copy to Senator Norris, who gave it his stamp of approval.

McNary was anxious to return to Oregon. He wrote his wife that receiving some pictures in the mail of her and Charlotte at

Fir Cone "made me so homesick I actually cried." He wrote his sister, "How happy I shall be to see you all, after nearly a years absence. And these years are precious jewels now because we are not getting any new supply, and those that remain are precious beyond calculation."

A solemn McNary (top), with Senate colleagues D. Worth Clark of Idaho and Tom Connally of Texas, announcing the death of Senator William E. Borah. McNary coordinated the funeral arrangements for his fellow western progressive.

In 1940, McNary, and GOP Senate colleagues Arthur Vandenberg and Robert A. Taft sought their party's presidential nomination (bottom). Senator Warren Austin of Vermont (on Taft's left) was running for re-election. (Both author's collection)

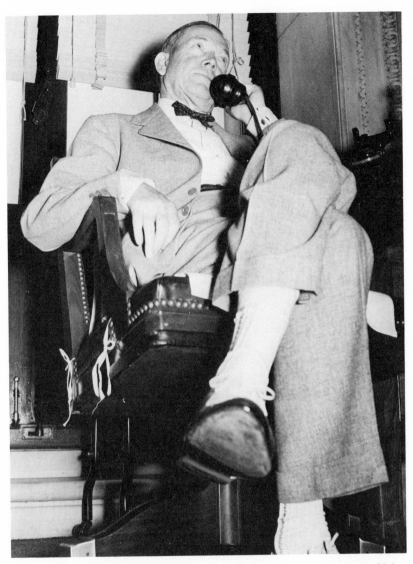

Leaning back in his leather chair, McNary was informed of his first-ballot nomination for the vice presidency in a telephone call from his Oregon friend Ralph Cake. (Author's collection)

On winning the vice-presidential nomination, McNary told reporters (top) that he had not wanted it, but would be "a good
soldier" in the interest of his party and home state.

Vice President Garner congratulated McNary (bottom) on his
nomination as Wendell Willkie's running-mate. Garner said that
the job wasn't worth a warm pitcher of spit and McNary called it
"a damn totem pole," but neither turned it down. (Both author's
collection)

Cornelia and Charlotte McNary were at Fir Cone during the
1940 Republican convention. (Author's collection)

In their first joint appearance as the 1940 Republican ticket, McNary lifted Willkie's arm in a gesture of victory. Even though their views differed on many issues and they had never met, Wendell L. Willkie chose McNary as his vice-presidential running-mate on the 1940 Republican ticket. In their first meeting, McNary advised Willkie to cut out the wisecracks because the public didn't vote for comedians. (Author's collection)

(Top) Prior to their nomination as running-mates on the 1940 Republican ticket, Willkie and McNary had never met.

(Bottom) Geography was a major consideration in Willkie's selection of McNary as his running-mate. (Berryman cartoons, both author's collection)

A 1940 Willkie-McNary poster. (Author's collection)

McNary (top) advised the thin-skinned Willkie not to be overly
concerned about Democratic campaign charges.

(Bottom) Normally cautious, McNary's early optimism about
Willkie's chances impressed such sympathetic observers as cartoonist C. K. Berryman. Privately, though, McNary acknowledged that FDR was almost unbeatable. (Both author's collection)

LIFE

McNARY OF OREGON

AUGUST 12, 1940 10 CENTS

McNary received cover treatment from *Life* magazine following his 1940 nomination for the vice-presidency. The senator didn't like the cover portrait but was pleased with Oregon writer Richard L. Neuberger's "Close-Up" profile. (Author's collection)

20

Candidate for Vice President

IT WAS MORE civic festival than political event. As Oregon's capital, Salem was accustomed to pomp and ceremony. But 27 August 1940 was something special, for the national political limelight was on the state fairgrounds. Charles L. McNary had come home to accept the Republican nomination for vice president.

Dark clouds threatened the ceremonies and yet thousands of people turned out anyway, including an official delegation of GOP leaders from each of the forty-eight states. The senator's portrait was given prominent display in the windows of every downtown storefront. Along the city's broad avenues, "Welcome McNary" signs were framed with red, white, and blue bunting. In anticipation of traffic jams and an overflow crowd, the fairgrounds were opened six hours before McNary's speech. Local merchants closed shop and state workers were let off early so that they would be assured of seats.

By noon, the sun had broken through and the crowd continued to build. It was the largest political audience in the city's history although there was some dispute about the actual count. The *Oregonian* and the Mutual Radio Network estimated the crowd at 40,000, while the *Oregon Journal* reported it was barely 12,000. Four national radio networks were carrying the program live, and Willkie listened on a portable radio in an Indianapolis coffee shop.

Before McNary's arrival, a dozen bands marched around the race track, playing, "There'll Be a Hot Time in the Old Town Tonight" and "Down by the Old Mill Stream." The proceedings were interrupted when seven black-robed demonstrators carrying anti-draft placards were ejected from the bleachers. The crowd cheered as someone ripped up a demonstrator's sign. There was another pause when a high school band member had an epileptic seizure. The Republican National Chairman Joe Martin and Minnesota Governor Harold Stassen received only polite applause for their preliminary remarks.

Entering the stadium in the back seat of an open car, McNary received a thunderous and prolonged ovation from his hometown audience. He was dressed in a gray suit with a red bow-tie and black-and-white shoes. When the cheering went on, McNary pulled his starched cuffs. Not until he raised both hands for silence did the crowd let him begin. The senator's voice was flat and undramatic but the speech demonstrated his notable literary style and outlined his political philosophy. McNary endorsed public power and a strong national defense. He acknowledged that the New Deal had been responsible for "certain social gains which have made the lot of the average man more secure." The senator declared, however, that too much power had been centralized in Washington during the Roosevelt years and called for shifting some responsibilities to the states. McNary ridiculed the statement by administration officials that America had moved from an era of growth into one of lowered expectations. "We of the Oregon country reject the hypothesis," he asserted. "We are optimists. We say that America is not yet half built."

After McNary's acceptance speech, it was reported that farm-belt movie audiences sat quietly during newsreel segments on FDR and Willkie but cheered and applauded when the Oregon senator appeared on the silver screen. In western states, McNary received equal billing with Willkie on campaign posters. "If McNary were the nominee for president and Willkie the nominee for vice president," said *Oregon Labor Press* editor Eugene Allen, "the Republicans would be a 100 percent better bet out this way."

McNary was receiving more public recognition than ever before. His face was splashed across the covers of *Life* and *Newsweek*, and he was the subject of a highly favorable profile by Joseph Alsop and Robert Kitner in the *Saturday Evening Post*. "I was pictured until I was almost paralyzed," McNary wrote his wife after one of his first appearances as the party's nominee. "I was quite unnerved."

Never a happy warrior on the stump, the Oregon senator did not look forward to hitting the trail. "I have no heart for the campaign, especially for a job I did not seek and care nothing about," McNary wrote his sister, "but I shall have to indulge in some of it, but no more than is absolutely necessary."

Willkie's strategists planned to use McNary in the Midwest and Far West, seeking to capitalize on his popularity in both regions. McNary said that he intended to let Willkie "carry the ball and set the pace," but agreed to do whatever his running-mate wanted. His first speech of the fall campaign was scheduled in Aurora, Illinois on 16 September 1940.

"I am trying to make a few appointments and am more particular about my speech than the number of speeches I shall make," he wrote Cornelia. "If I were knocking about the country like Mr. Willkie with a special train and all, I would, of course, insist that you be along. But I am not doing that, nor do I think it is proper for me to do so as I am not a candidate for the first position. Therefore, my excursion into the country will be sporadic, that is, one at a time, and then return to Washington for several days."

With the coming of the television age, vice-presidential campaign entourages would become larger. But in 1940, McNary traveled with a single political aide, Forrest Davis, and few if any reporters. On several occasions, McNary and Wallace rode on the same train and had their meals together. Though they were opponents, the two men genuinely liked each other and did not hesitate to say so publicly. During his Oregon swing, Wallace said that McNary was "best loved of all the United States Senate." And when Wallace linked Willkie with Wall Street financial interests, he interjected, "Senator McNary has no such connections." For his part, McNary hailed Wallace as a "high-minded and sympathetic Secretary of Agriculture."

McNary's campaign tactics were a far cry from the slashing body attacks that would become a trademark of later GOP vice-presidential nominees. "I have never been a violent party man," the Oregon senator told a midwestern audience. "I don't know if I should be the vice-presidential candidate," McNary confided to Carlton Savage. "I'm not enough of a partisan."

But McNary sounded very much like a Republican candidate in his Aurora, Illinois appearance. He berated Wallace for declaring that the GOP was the "party of appeasement." "To suggest that Republicans are eager to appease Hitler, with the blood of the European democracies fresh on his hands, is, of course, an irresponsible generalization unworthy of a leader in times of tension." McNary charged, "The New Deal's failure with an America at peace disqualified it for administering the affairs of an America that may be at war." He asserted that Willkie "would galvanize the nation into an intensified effort that would shortly spell security against any foe."

Following this speech, McNary wrote his sister, "I had a nice crowd, attentive and appreciative. I may have spoken as though I was hoarse once or twice, but that was because I was over straining my voice to accommodate a maladjusted set-up of amplifier and microphone. But I did not hurry at all. I was deliberate and did not feel at all disturbed or nervous."

McNary tacitly approved FDR's destroyers-for-bases deal with Winston Churchill in the late summer. The British prime minister had asked Roosevelt for fifty World War I destroyers to help defend Britain against Nazi Germany, and, at the same time, proposed turning over British bases to the U.S. in the Caribbean. Since the transaction would be in violation of the arms embargo, McNary advised the White House that he would find it difficult to support legislation approving the deal. But the Senate minority leader said that he would make no objection if FDR invoked his emergency powers and sent Britain the warships and obtained the bases on grounds of national security. With McNary's support, Roosevelt did just that. Willkie, who approved of the deal with legislation, called it "the most dictatorial and arbitrary act of any president in the history of the United States."

McNary also gave Roosevelt important support on the nation's first peacetime draft. The Selective Service legislation had been sponsored by Senator Edward Burke, a conservative Nebraska Democrat, and Congressman James W. Wadsworth, a New York Republican. On 12 August 1940, FDR wrote a Democratic congressman who had suggested that the president meet with Willkie to issue a bipartisan agreement on the draft. "He has no desire to cooperate and is merely playing politics," Roosevelt wrote. "I am inclined to think that the best approach is an appeal to the patriotism of Joe Martin and Charlie McNary." Martin had urged Willkie not to endorse the draft, but the Republican presidential candidate urged passage of the Selective Service Act as "the only democratic way in which to secure the trained and competent manpower we need for national defense." McNary gave the bill his backing, and it was passed and signed in October.

After making an appearance with Willkie at Forbes Field in Pittsburgh, McNary declined when Martin asked to campaign in other eastern cities. "Listen, Joe, suppose you just let me talk to the farmers," the Oregon senator told the GOP national chairman. "Every time I show up for a speech in a big town, the Chamber of Commerce and businessmen take over the meeting. They want to be helpful. But I feel like a stuffed shirt talking about the farm question in a setting like that. I'll make more votes for the ticket if I confine my campaigning to small communities and agricultural centers, where I can do some down-to-earth talking with farmers."

McNary's next campaign swing was through the farm belt. In Minnesota, he gave the keynote address at the Red River Valley corn show. In Iowa, he paid tribute to his old friend Gilbert Haugen in the late congressman's hometown of Northwood. McNary was introduced by Haugen's daughter, and he spoke with deeply felt emotion of the McNary-Haugen farm relief battles. "The proposals established a principle that later found favor," he said. "That principle was that the farmer deserved some relief from the disadvantages pressed upon him by the tariff and his subserviency to world market prices. It has been honored in certain parts of New Deal farm legislation. The principle—although never invoked—may be said to be a sort of monument to the work of Gilbert Haugen and his associates." McNary pledged to continue fighting for his late colleagues goal—equality for the farmer. In Kansas, McNary alleged that the Roosevelt administration's trade policies were hurting the farmer and called for legislation that would protect "the American market for the American farmer." In Missouri, he linked FDR with corrupt big city Democratic machines and charged that "third-term partisans" were seeking to build "township Tammanys" by manipulating aid to farmers.

While he preferred the farm belt to the Northeast, McNary continued to regard campaigning as an ordeal. "I shall feel as happy as a pardoned prisoner when it is all over," he wrote his wife. "I should be happy if I were heading homeward." he told his sister. "The home-minded man has no business chasing around the country, but sometimes events are thrust upon us in such a fashion that we cannot follow our own course."

From the beginning of the fall campaign, McNary doubted whether Willkie could defeat FDR. "I am not setting any eggs on the results," he wrote Ella in late September. "It seems inconceivable that the Republicans can beat the war in Europe and the $15 million now being expended in all matters of enterprises, including reliefers, farm bonuses, and war activities. But the family historian can say that it was a nice experience, while the rest of us can sit around the fireplace at Fir Cone or a hot-air stove at the Poor Farm and reflect on the philosophy that privacy has more charm than publicity."

One month later, he was slightly more optimistic when Willkie's aggressive campaigning forced Roosevelt to abandon his Rose Garden strategy and polls showed the race tightening. "Our party is making inroads," McNary wrote his wife on 20 October. "We have a fair chance, but the odds are so great. We must fight a war and billions of dollars in benefit payments. My chief interest lies in doing the best I can. I have been repaid by the vast numbers of people I have seen and their earnestness and belief in my integrity."

Ending his campaign in the Far West, McNary delivered speeches in Salt Lake City and Sacramento before heading north to Salem. McNary called for a revival of the pioneer spirit and rejection of "the New Deal creed that we are an aging people, ready to give up the struggle" for an expanding economy. "Whatever goes on the following Tuesday, it will be perfectly all right with me," he wrote Ella. "So I do not want any of you folks stirred up and thinking that I shall feel bad if the ultimate is not attained—not at all."

On election eve, McNary spoke to the nation in a radio broadcast from his farm. "The New Deal, which assumed power when our forces had been demoralized by a world economic crisis, organized a retreat. The fault I charge now is that the New Deal continued to retreat from our traditions, taking deeper and deeper refuge in paternalism and stateism. Tomorrow we must decide whether this retreat shall go on." The nation cannot exist, McNary said, "half prosperous, half depressed."

McNary and Cornelia cast their ballots the next morning in the Chemama Grange Hall. In the afternoon, they began listening to the election returns from the East with McNary's Oregon relatives in the living room at Fir Cone. Across the country, Willkie awaited the outcome in his New York headquarters at the Commodore Hotel, and FDR monitored the election in the study of his mansion at Hyde Park. Roosevelt was concerned when Willkie surged in the early returns and moved ahead in New York, but the president relaxed when he carried his home state by 224,000 votes. Although Willkie and McNary received more votes than any ticket in the GOP's history, it wasn't enough. They scored a near-sweep of the Midwest but were losing everywhere else. McNary's presence on the ticket resulted in Roosevelt's smallest margin in Oregon of his four campaigns, but the president still carried the state. McNary thought Willkie looked petty in refusing to concede defeat when the results were obvious. So the Oregon senator made his own concession statement shortly before Willkie went to bed. "I am congratulating Mr. Roosevelt and Mr. Wallace and wishing them grace and their administration prosperity," said McNary. "We are a united country. The two-party system is secure. We shall try to afford Mr. Roosevelt and his associates a worthy and vigilant opposition."

"Many thanks for your generous and therefore characteristic message," FDR wired McNary from Hyde Park. "I know you and I will work together in the national interest. I heartily reciprocate all your good wishes."

McNary received bushels of mail from supporters and friends. "I doubt if any candidate for president of the United States ever had such a congenial and capable running mate as I had," wrote Willkie. Walter Lippmann wrote McNary, "You are a gallant gentleman." McNary's 1936 opponent, Willis Mahoney, wrote, "you have emerged from this campaign with the respect and admiration of the American people. Your gentlemanly conduct, your tolerance, your deep devotion to American ideals holds the admiration of everyone."

Robert S. Allen and Drew Pearson reported that FDR was giving consideration to naming McNary as the next secretary of agriculture to succeed Wallace who was moving into the vice presidency. Allen and Pearson said that Roosevelt wanted to bring another prominent Republican into the cabinet because the threat of war would require bipartisanship in all fields. George Putnam, editor of the Salem *Capital Journal*, wrote that there was no doubt about McNary's qualifications. "But," Putnam argued, "the senator is too valuable to Oregon in the Senate, and to the Republican party as Senate leader to justify an acceptance of the cabinet post if tendered."

"Nothing to it," McNary wrote his executive secretary. "Of course, you know I would not take the position under these circumstances or any other so far as I know. I have no fear but that I could handle it with technique and a little skill but I would not throw my party down."

McNary could have had the cabinet slot for the asking. But he was not interested in leaving the Senate leadership for a job he had declined in earlier administrations. The senator told Ralph Cake that Roosevelt had clinched his third term in June when the Nazi conquest of France had the effect of making FDR a wartime president.

In late November, McNary was hospitalized with pneumonia following a visit to Timberline Lodge. Exhausted and weak, he spent Christmas with his family at Fir Cone and then embarked for a resort in California's Mohave Desert where he sought to recover his strength. Now that the campaign was over, McNary looked forward to returning to the work he liked best.

In his first transcontinental flight, McNary left the nation's capitol to accept the vice-presidential nomination in his hometown. (Author's collection)

OREGON'S
OWN SON!

Charles L.

McNARY

IS OUR NEXT
VICE-PRESIDENT

Arriving in Portland (top), McNary was greeted by his daughter Charlotte and his wife, Cornelia.

(Bottom) McNary may have been number two on the 1940 GOP ticket, but he got top billing in his home state. (Both author's collection)

At the conclusion of his acceptance speech, McNary acknowledged the tumultuous ovation from his hometown audience at the Oregon Fairgrounds. (Author's collection)

McNary accepts the warm applause of a home-state audience during the 1940 campaign. (Author's collection)

McNary's 1940 Democratic opponent for the vice-presidency was Secretary of Agriculture Henry A. Wallace (opposite page, top), who got his political start campaigning for McNary's farm-relief legislation in the 1920s. When they mentioned each other on the stump, McNary and Wallace accentuated the positive, a rarity in national politics.

(Opposite page, bottom) McNary's presence on the Republican ticket was considered a major asset to midwestern GOP candidates whose political fortunes were linked to the farm vote. In Illinois, Dwight Green (left), a former U.S. attorney who had successfully prosecuted gangster Al Capone for tax evasion, was elected governor, and C. Wayland Brooks was elected to the U.S. Senate with McNary's help in the farm belt.

In one of their rare joint appearances (above), Willkie and McNary spoke at a labor rally in Pittsburgh. (All author's collection)

On election day, McNary voted early at the Keizer Grange Hall and awaited the nation's verdict at Fir Cone. Though polls had shown the GOP ticket gaining ground in the final days of the campaign, the Oregon senator had few illusions about their chances against FDR. (Author's collection)

21

World War II

BACK IN WASHINGTON, McNary was among the few prominent Republicans who pressed for "an all-out policy of aid to
the democracies by every method short of war." The debate
over FDR's lend-lease bill was reaching a climax. With Britain
running low on cash to pay for American weaponry, Roosevelt
was seeking to replace the U.S. cash-and-carry policy with immediate emergency loans. "Give us the tools," thundered Churchill, "and we'll finish the job." In a Fireside Chat, FDR compared lend-lease to lending a garden hose to a neighbor whose
home was on fire. Roosevelt said that it was common sense to
lend the hose and ask for its return once the fire had been put
out. The isolationists argued that it was a step toward war. The
Chicago Tribune denounced it as the "war dictatorship bill," and
the *New York Daily News*, which had been a staunch FDR supporter, broke permanently with the administration on this issue. Senators Wheeler, Taft, and Vandenberg were strongly
against it as were Herbert Hoover, Alf M. Landon, Norman
Thomas, and Colonel Charles A. Lindbergh.

McNary thought the isolationists were risking disaster in attempting to block all forms of lend-lease. At the same time, he
believed that the bill's original version granted too much authority to the chief executive. Late in January, the Oregon senator conferred with FDR and found him willing to accept legislation with some of the revisions McNary wanted. "I am sure a

united country is better than one separated on an issue so important," the senator wrote privately.

"Everything here is the Lend-Lease bill," McNary wrote his sister. "It's a mess. I am occupying a middle position between the Willkieites and anti-Willkieites, the interventionists and the noninterventionists, the isolationists and the internationalists. Of course, there will be people in the state who won't be satisfied with my vote, but I'll follow Pinnochio's advice and let my conscience be my guide."

McNary showed political courage in making his decision. Two-thirds of the Republican senators and most of his party's national leadership were flatly opposed to lend-lease, but McNary recognized the importance of aid to Britain. "I shall vote for the bill with the present amendments," he wrote his sister on 28 February 1941. "I have given the matter much thought and I believe the surest way for us to protect our country's future is by assisting in squelching Mr. Hitler now."

On 7 March 1941, the Senate approved lend-lease. Senator Hiram Johnson, a bitter isolationist, wrote his son, "The severest blow came when McNary went back on us." Senator Vandenberg wrote in his diary: "If America 'cracks up', you can put your finger on this precise moment as the time when the crime was committed. I had the feeling, as the result of the ballot was announced, that I was witnessing the suicide of the republic." McNary had no regrets about his controversial vote. "I did what I thought was right," said the Oregon Republican.

Like many Americans, McNary had been preoccupied with the Great Depression in the Thirties and had underestimated the threat of Nazi Germany. The Oregon senator had never traveled outside of North America and had little understanding of the forces that were overtaking Europe. "I do not think there will be a European War," McNary wrote a constituent on 2 June 1939.

Three months later, Hitler invaded Poland and went to war against France and Britain. FDR asked Congress for repeal of the neutrality act, especially the arms embargo against all belligerents. McNary agreed to help Roosevelt get a quick vote on the arms embargo, although he opposed the president's approach. "The trouble is that people would think, if we repealed the whole neutrality act," said McNary, "that we were repealing our neutrality." The Oregon Republican wrote privately, "I fear if we send munitions to belligerents they may be followed by money and then by men. We have no business in becoming involved in the European mess that has been going on for a thousand years. Further, we got mixed up twenty years ago and the tragic results are known to all." In November, with McNary and most Senate Republicans in opposition, FDR managed to get repeal of the arms embargo.

It took Germany only three weeks to defeat Poland. Then, for the next eight months, there was so little action on the European front that a great many Americans shared William E. Borah's view that it was a "phony war." On 10 May 1940 that illusion was shattered when Hitler's stormtroopers charged into France and the Low Countries. "For some time the European war has looked gloomy from the standpoint of the Allies," McNary wrote his sister, "and now a good many of the political leaders about Washington are considering peace in terms of Germany's stipulations."

McNary, who abhorred Hitler and now recognized his threat to the United States, gave FDR support to put the nation on a war footing. He voted for the first peacetime draft and tacitly supported the destroyer-bases deal with Great Britain. He and George Norris were the only Republican progressives who voted for lend-lease aid to Britain. "The war abroad and its implications here have cast a dark shadow over Congress and everything is talk of war abroad or prospects for war here," he wrote his sister on 9 May 1941. "We may get in. I have not thought so, but am beginning to think it is probable. If we get in, I think it is because Mr. Hitler wants to fight, not because we are discreet. But I don't think he wants to fight."

After spending the summer at Fir Cone, the Oregon senator was more optimistic that Americans might be spared another world war. "In my opinion, Hitlerism reached its peak a year ago," he wrote Cornelia in September, "and is now traveling toward the setting sun." But, a month later the senator wrote his niece: "It is possible this president will take us into this cruel war conflict. The only thing that will keep us out will be that Hitler and Japan refuse to fight. There is no good purpose in discussing that lurid situation, but I still believe we won't get into it and that the thing will be over within the next year."

In November, McNary fought Roosevelt's effort to revise the neutrality act so that armed American ships could carry lend-lease materials to the British. The Senate minority leader worried that it could force an incident that would bring the U.S.

into the war. "If Mr. Hitler and his allies want to fight," he wrote, "they will have justification to do so."

Willkie called for repealing the neutrality act and got McNary's assistant floor leader, Warren Austin of Vermont, to sponsor such legislation. The 1940 GOP presidential candidate angered McNary in recruiting several of the senator's closest political allies back in Oregon to come out for repeal, including Governor Sprague, Ralph Cake, and Republican state chairman Neil Allen. On 7 November the Senate narrowly approved repeal of restrictive sections of the neutrality act.

McNary was stunned to learn of the surprise Japanese attack on Pearl Harbor on 7 December 1941. Half of the Navy's Pacific fleet had been wiped out. "I did not expect this sudden turn of events," McNary wrote his sister, "and it was rather a shock. The whole thing looks to me now as though we would become involved in the greater world war, not only with Japan but also with her Axis partners, Germany and Italy."

The Senate minority leader was among the handful of friends and advisers who were immediately summoned to the White House after the shocking news. McNary stood directly behind FDR as the president signed the declarations of war against the Axis powers. The Oregon senator pledged the unanimous support of the Republican minority behind Roosevelt's prosecution of the war. As far as he and his colleagues were concerned, McNary told the president that politics were adjourned. In private, McNary blamed Roosevelt for maneuvering the nation toward war. "It is true that when we get a Democratic administration," he wrote Ray Gill, "we get into a world war. Maybe it is to cover their domestic sins."

"Indignation runs high here in connection with the disaster in Pearl Harbor," McNary wrote his sister five days after the Japanese attack. "The tragedy was wholly avoidable. The capitol battleships were sitting on the water much like decoy ducks on a calm lake."

"Our first duty now," McNary told Ella, "is to knock down the ears of those little yellow rats of the Orient." Like most of his contemporaries among the western progressives, McNary retained some of his small-town prejudices. Although generous to the blacks who served on his Senate staff, he was not interested in civil rights issues and privately accused FDR of "playing at all times with the colored vote." The senator wrote his sister late in 1942, "The war will end someday and so will the Roosevelts, and then the colored people will be willing again to work as domestics." McNary jolted an Interior Department official, according to Harold Ickes, by asking "whether we had any white men (meaning other than Jews), with whom he could deal." Yet McNary strongly disapproved of the public anti-semitism of a Corvallis editor who was active in Oregon Republican party affairs. Deeply touched by the plight of European Jews, McNary became national co-chairman with Senator Robert Wagner of a committee supporting the establishment of a Jewish homeland in Palestine.

In the early months of 1942, there was little encouraging news about the war. The Americans were being routed in the Pacific. MacArthur fled the Philippines and the Japanese captured Singapore. The British were losing in North Africa, and the Soviets were under siege from Hitler's armies. While McNary gave Roosevelt public support, he was privately critical of the administration's handling of the war, describing the nation's capital as "an overgrown mess due to war activities, boondoggling, extravagence and waste of the New Deal and associates."

McNary was a friend and admirer of General George C. Marshall, the Army's chief of staff, whom he had known since Marshall was the brigadier general in charge of the old Fort Vancouver barracks. In choosing Marshall as organizer of the war effort, McNary thought FDR had found the right man for the monumental task.

The Senate minority leader did not share FDR's infatuation with Churchill. After meeting the British prime minister at the White House, McNary wrote his sister that while Churchill had been "interesting," he "made a very lame excuse for the English defeat in Libya." McNary went on, "Titles are as thick about here as ticks in the woods of Eastern Oregon. I suspect they are all after money. But the fellow that is dangerous in that line is Churchill. He has a great influence over the gentleman at the White House and he would carry off the White House if it were not difficult to put inside a plane."

Seldom offering any public comments on the progress of the war, McNary expressed strong views in his correspondence. He thought Churchill was wrong and Stalin right on the need for a second front in Europe during 1942. "I am a little concerned about the war in Russia," he wrote his sister. "If Russia caves in, I do not see how we can dislodge Mr. Hitler. We may have to have an armed truce for years." McNary thought that FDR overestimated the worth of battleships and should put more emphasis on air power. "We need more planes to hold our own and win this war," he wrote in March. "But for home folks, let me say that the President is wedded to the old battleship as my grandfather was to the covered wagon and father to the horse and buggy and refuses to become air-minded." In September of 1942, McNary wrote Cornelia, "If we could get the old brass hats and braids air-minded, we could whip Hitler and Japan with our planes and save most of our men."

By the spring of 1942, the Americans had struck back at Japan. Major General Jimmy Doolittle's planes bombed Tokyo. The Americans defeated the Japanese in the battles of the Coral Sea and Midway, and the U.S. Marines would soon occupy Guadalcanal after some of the bloodiest fighting of the war.

McNary and other congressional leaders had minimal influence on wartime policy. But Roosevelt continued to rely on him as the Senate's most effective conciliator in matters concerning the home front. When the president's call for price controls touched off a political explosion, it was McNary who worked out the compromise anti-inflation measure that gained unanimous approval.

Always attentive to his home state, McNary used his position to make certain that Oregon received its share of federal war projects. Through the senator's efforts, the Tongue Point naval station was built at the mouth of the Columbia. At a cabinet meeting, FDR announced that "Charley McNary's price" for the Naval appropriation bill was a patrol boat for the Columbia, and the president went along. McNary and Ickes pushed through FDR's bill for the Bonneville Power Administration over an alternative plan sponsored by Senator Homer Bone of Washington and Norris that would have required three commissioners instead of one administrator.

McNary was running for his fifth term in 1942, announcing his candidacy more than a year before the election. Although he had nearly been defeated in the 1936 FDR landslide and had failed to carry Oregon as the vice-presidential nominee in 1940, McNary was considered just about unbeatable this time because of the war and his prominence as the state's only national political figure. Even Willis Mahoney, who had been his most formidable opponent, endorsed him for re-election in 1942.

Without an official endorsement, the White House made it known that FDR ardently supported McNary's re-election. "No one holds him in higher esteem and warmer personal affection than Franklin Roosevelt," reported Drew Pearson. "Despite the fact that McNary is the leader of the opposition party, he is one of the president's most trusted advisers. Only insiders know it, but Roosevelt consults McNary more frequently than certain Democratic leaders." Richard L. Neuberger wrote in the *Progressive* that FDR wanted McNary retained as the Senate's Republican leader because any successor would be "far more personal, far more acrimonious and far more frequently in opposition."

McNary was challenged in the primary by a political gadfly named Arthur M. Geary who said that the overriding issue of the campaign was "MacArthurism versus McNaryism." The senator's polls showed him winning renomination by almost five-to-one, and in the May primary, those figures proved to be accurate. "It was a swell victory," McNary wrote his sister. "I was not much scared about the results, but I got sore inwardly at the unfairness of the pup. I was afraid he would mislead the people in these dislocated times because everyone had grievances about something occasioned by the conduct of the war or disturbances caused to the orthodox way of living."

Confident of the fall election, McNary did not bother to return for any campaigning. Several weeks before the midterm elections, Roosevelt honored McNary in asking whether he would be interested in going on the Supreme Court of the United States. The President confided that he would soon have a vacancy because James F. Byrnes was leaving the high court to become presidential assistant for economic affairs. But McNary was not interested. "Very confidentially, the White House sounded me out," the senator wrote his sister, "and I said 'no'. I would not be happy writing opinions based on what some old judge said in the threadbare past. This life is too active, and my position is too important to give up at this time because when the war is over, the United States Senate under the Constitution will have to write the treaties of peace. For that work, I think, I am fitted."

As expected, McNary easily defeated Democrat Walter W. Whitbeck, winning seventy-seven percent of the vote and a plurality of more than 150,000 votes. "I probably will quit running, if they don't break the old picture, in about 1969," McNary wrote Ella, "and I shall be old enough to retire to Fir Cone.":

It was a Republican year nationally as well. The GOP gained ten seats in the Senate and forty-seven in the House of Representatives. Thomas E. Dewey of New York and Earl Warren of California were among the newly elected Republican governors. "This is only a breeze compared with what will happen in 1944," McNary predicted. The Oregon senator was saddened by the defeat of Norris, his longtime ally from Nebraska, who had sought re-election as an independent and lost to Republican Kenneth Wherry. McNary told Ickes that the Democratic setbacks "were due to the people's dissatisfaction with the operation of the war program."

Speaking on the floor of the Senate two days after the election, Democratic Senator Tom Connally of Texas voiced his concern that the nation's enemies might misinterpret the administration's setbacks in the midterm elections. McNary jumped to his feet and berated Connally, saying there was no way "that our adversaries in this global war could possibly misconceive the results of the election" since "no issue of patriotism or unity was raised."

"Many times," McNary declared, "I have felt like raising my voice in opposition to some things which I thought were major mistakes. I persuaded myself it was better for our country and our unity to withhold criticism. I intend to continue." McNary said that the American people had grown tired of "the ever-increasing number of commissions and czars and dictators." He also criticized the administration's "wastage of public funds." McNary concluded, "If the recent election causes our friends in control to be more careful with funds, it will have been a grand victory."

It was McNary's sharpest rebuke of the war, one of the few times that he had gone public with his misgivings about the administration's handling of the war. "For a year I have been approaching the point where I thought I could speak up and speak out without being accused of playing politics or favoring Hitler, or being in the employ of the Japs," McNary wrote his sister. "This wicked New Deal propaganda machine likes to tear men down, but, frankly, I do not think they will tackle me. I think the vote last Tuesday will settle this bunch of bluffers and incompetents. I had no intention of speaking out so boldly in the Senate, but the Democrats started the argument and without preparation I gave them my views."

By the end of 1942, the Nazis were on the defensive. Hitler had lost the battle of Stalingrad and his gamble for the Soviet Union. Rommel, the legendary Desert Fox, had been defeated by the allies in North Africa. The Americans and British were bombing Germany and Italy. McNary was already thinking in terms of writing the peace treaties for the postwar era.

Soon after the 1940 election, McNary relaxed at Timberline Lodge on Mount Hood. Here (top) he is descending the famous "Magic Mile" chairlift from Silcox Hut.

(Bottom) Sharing a ride to the White House with Vice President John Nance Garner and Senate Majority Leader Alben Barkley. (Both author's collection)

McNary and congressional leaders stood behind FDR as he signed the declaration of war against Japan on the day after the attack on Pearl Harbor. The others are House Speaker Sam Rayburn, House Majority Leader John W. McCormack, Senate Majority Leader Barkley, and Senator Carter Glass of Virginia. (Author's collection)

McNary played a key role in the U.S. decision to send destroyers to aid the embattled British in 1940 and was among the few
prominent Republicans to support lend-lease legislation. But he
considered Prime Minister Winston Churchill something of a
windbag. In the spring of 1943, McNary, Barkley, Vice President
Henry Wallace and House Speaker Rayburn shared the stage
with the British statesman as he addressed a joint session of Congress. (Author's collection)

On his final visit to Oregon (top), in the fall of 1943, McNary was honored at an Albany luncheon.

More than a thousand mourners attended funeral services for McNary at the Oregon statehouse (bottom), including twenty-six of his U.S. Senate colleagues. (Both author's collection)

(Top) In 1954, President Dwight D. Eisenhower dedicated the Columbia River dam in the senator's memory. (Author's collection)

(Bottom) Long-time *Oregonian* political cartoonist Quincy Scott's farewell tribute to Charles L. McNary, 27 February 1944. (Both author's collection)

22

The Last Progressive

ONCE THE WAR had ended, Senator McNary did not want the nation to go through an encore of the polarizing struggle over Wilson's League. As one of the few survivors of that bitter political battle, McNary took it upon himself to work with his Senate colleagues and FDR in helping avoid the mistakes that had doomed the Versailles Treaty. "I am trying to smother fires that are being fanned to prevent conflagration involving isolationism and internationalism," he wrote Ella in January of 1943. "I hope I am successful and believe that I shall be."

McNary declared that, while Senate Republicans were in favor of international cooperation, they were against massive foreign aid programs and trade concessions that put American producers at a disadvantage in the marketplace. "We should look at the subject realistically," the Oregon senator wrote privately about postwar treaties, "and not be a bunch of suckers all the time."

In the middle of March, McNary joined Secretary of State Cordell Hull and Tom Connally, chairman of the Senate Foreign Relations Committee, in drafting a compromise resolution which would commit the United States to membership in an international peace organization. The resolution called for the complete defeat of the Axis powers and advocated "participation by the United States in the creation and maintenance of an international organization to insure permanent peace." It would be months before the Senate would be asked to take action on the resolution. "The matter had to be handled," recalled Hull, "with extreme care and delicacy, lest it revive old controversies."

McNary was politically embarrassed in July when Hull announced that the Senate minority leader and other congressional leaders had said that the United States should participate in the United Nations organization through executive order. When Vandenberg wired McNary in protest, the Oregon senator insisted that he had made no such commitment. "So sure as the sun shines over the mountains, our distinguished president never discussed with me the terms or conditions contained in any of the so-called UN Relief or Rehabilitation draft agreements." McNary said that his discussions with FDR had been in general terms, with no final agreement between them.

"Unless the peace after this war is to be as unstable as was that after the last war, planning must be started now," McNary declared from Fir Cone in August, "but no blueprint defining the course of this nation can be made until the people as a whole can express themselves. I believe the men now at the front should be consulted before the final decisions are made. I want to know what the soldiers and the people want, and what is in the minds of leaders such as Churchill and Stalin before I commit myself to a plan."

McNary was invited but did not attend the mid-September Republican conference on Mackinac Island, between Lake Michigan and Lake Huron, where forty-nine party leaders endorsed U.S. membership in a postwar organization "among sovereign nations to prevent military aggression and to attain permanent peace with organized justice in a free world." McNary was more than satisfied with the resolution and predicted that the Senate would vote overwhelmingly in favor of American participation in the United Nations.

In the middle of October, FDR invited McNary to accompany him on a planned trip to the Pacific Northwest. "I could see some politics in that," McNary wrote his sister, "and told him I doubted if I could go on a trip with him." Although he was nearly seventy, McNary's name was periodically mentioned as a possible Republican candidate for the presidency in 1944. But when a group of home state supporters announced plans to file petitions entering McNary in the Oregon presidential primary, McNary said that he would not be a candidate. In the fall of 1943, the Mississippi legislature approved a resolution which endorsed a Roosevelt-McNary unity ticket for the 1944 election.

McNary had soured on Willkie, his 1940 running mate, and it was against the senator's advice that his old friend Ralph Cake became national campaign manager of Willkie's 1944 comeback bid. *Time* publisher Henry Luce had a long talk with McNary, hoping to neutralize his opposition to Willkie, but the senator was unpersuaded. When *Look* magazine helped launch Willkie's campaign with a special issue and national advertising describing him as "Another Lincoln," McNary was outraged. "He launched a tirade against the *Look* advertisements," recalled John D.M. Hamilton, "saying that no man with a reasonable income could hope to be president of the United States if he had to combat advertisements to the extent of $300,000 to $400,000 which were charged to business." McNary told Hamilton, who was leading a stop-Willkie movement, that Willkie would probably win the Oregon primary. "You fellows better get a candidate," the Oregon senator advised Hamilton, "or you can bet Willkie will be nominated."

For months, McNary had been in ill health. He looked frail and tired, and his robust complexion had turned gray. "I am still weak," he wrote Ella in March of 1943. "I do not seem to bounce back like the rubber ball I used to be." At Fir Cone, his friends and neighbors were struck by the difference in his appearance since his previous visit nearly two years earlier. He no longer walked with his youthful bounce and he complained frequently of headaches. Back in Washington in September, McNary wrote his wife, "The work here seems dreary, dry and drab and I cannot get in the swing of all the mess, misery and moronic mechanism. It seems I was more wedded to home's pleasant surroundings than ever and why one should hang around public life is beginning to dawn upon me as a display of Neanderthal nonsense."

His condition grew worse and McNary knew something was wrong. He had always spoken precisely and yet he was beginning to slur his words and forget a thought in mid-sentence. "I have had a little dullness in the head for some time," he wrote his sister on 22 October. "I do not have any pains, but I have a kind of dizzy head with slow-working brains and dumbness in recalling words and names." One week later, he reported to Ella, "I do not find any aches other than in the head. My head seems to be a little dizzy, vacant, tired and full of aches. What I think is the matter is the result of the long years of work and responsibility which have more or less worn me out in the nerves and in the head, and I shall take a little spare time between now and the first of the year. So I am going to a lot of trouble to look after myself because there are a lot of things to do before I get ready to build my house among the mansions in the sky."

On 8 November, McNary checked into the U.S. Naval Hospital in Bethesda. When the doctors took X-rays, they found that McNary had a brain tumor. Within a week, the senator underwent surgery. The neurosurgeons later told Harold Ickes that the malignancy "had spread pretty much throughout the brain and was beyond correction." McNary was released from the hospital on 2 December 1943, and the bulletins from his office indicated that he was recovering. McNary's doctors said privately that he did not have long to live.

McNary looked gaunt and pale as he embarked for Florida from Washington's Union Station in early December. The senator and his family spent the winter in an oceanfront resort at Fort Lauderdale. By January, McNary had recovered enough strength to take short walks along the beach with his daughter, and he spoke of returning to Washington and resuming his duties. But his doctor insisted that he needed another month of rest. On 24 February 1944, the Senate's Republicans unanimously re-elected McNary as their leader and chairman of the party conference, but he had slipped into a coma and never got the news. With Cornelia and her sister May Morton at his side, McNary died the next afternoon.

Across the nation, the senator's death was mourned. "He possessed besides a delightful personality, rare gifts of statesmanship," FDR wrote McNary's widow. "As minority leader of the Senate, he put the national interest above blind partisanship and was ever free of rancor or intolerance. I counted Charles McNary among my real friends and I shall miss his companionship and his helpful cooperation in essential things."

Lord Halifax, the British ambassador in Washington, wrote his government, "With the death of Senator McNary, the Republicans have lost their ablest parliamentarian and one of the strongest influences in the party." Senator Robert A. Taft declared, "The Senate and the Republican party cannot replace his judgment, calm impartialty and able leadership." Another Republican senator observed that McNary's death was "the worst thing which has happened to the Republican party since it lost the presidency in 1932."

Vice President Henry A. Wallace remembered McNary as "one of the finest men I have ever known. He joined with my father in fighting for agricultural justice against the leaders of his own party." Interior Secretary Ickes wrote in his diary, "McNary's loss is a serious one. He exerted great influence in the Senate, both as minority leader and in his own personal right. He was never a bitter partisan. He supported or opposed measures, generally speaking, on their merit and not for political purposes. . . . From the point of view of the public power situation in the far Northwest, his loss is an irreparable one."

Former Oregon Governor Charles A. Sprague wrote, "He will be remembered not for any pomp or ceremony which attended him, but for his own intimate self, kindly, genial, helpful." State Senator Coe McKenna wrote a national party leader about McNary's death, "Our local political situation has been materially upset by the death of Senator McNary. His loss removes the one influential national factor from the whole Pacific area and unfortunately replacement is impossible. We have no man of prominence in political life who would be even comparable."

McNary's flag-draped coffin was shipped across the country by train. More than a thousand people attended his state funeral in the Oregon capitol, including twenty-six members of the U.S. Senate. He was buried on a gentle slope overlooking his hometown.

Richard L. Neuberger described him as one of the last progressives of the great tradition, and McNary's death symbolized the passing of an era. But he had left a rich legacy. His leadership in forest conservation had been responsible for protection of the nation's natural treasures. William B. Greeley, the former chief of the Forest Service, said that McNary had done more for forestry than any senator in the nation's history. His efforts for farm relief focused attention on the problems of rural America and resulted in farm parity. He was the father of power development in the Columbia river that helped bring the Pacific Northwest into the modern era. In a turbulent era, Charles Linza McNary was among the few national legislators who truly counted.

Bibliographical Essay

MOST OF SENATOR McNary's official and personal files are in the Charles L. McNary collection in the Manuscripts Division of the Library of Congress. Spanning the period from 1921 to 1944, it includes letters, family correspondence, speeches, newspaper clippings and legislative files. McNary's family provided me with several trunks of material that had previously been unavailable to scholars. The University of Oregon and Oregon Historical Society have much smaller but useful collections of McNary material. The Thomas Neuhausen, Henry Hanzen, Oswald West, and Richard Neuberger manuscripts at the University of Oregon were helpful. The Franklin D. Roosevelt and Herbert Hoover presidential libraries both contain much relevant material on McNary and his times. The Wendell L. Willkie papers in Indiana University's Lilly Library are especially useful for background on McNary's role as the 1940 Republican vice-presidential candidate. So, too, were the John D.M. Hamilton, Robert A. Taft, Raymond Clapper, Felix Frankfurter and Joseph Alsop papers in the Library of Congress.

Among the unpublished appraisals of McNary's public career are Howard A. DeWitt, "Charles L. McNary: His Early Political Career," University of Oregon, 1967; Roger T. Johnson, "Charles L. McNary and the Republican Party," University of Wisconsin, 1967; Walter K. Roberts, "The Political Career of Charles L. McNary," University of North Carolina, 1954, George Hoffmann, "The Early Political Career of Charles McNary," University of Southern California, 1951; and John David Phillips, "Charles L. McNary: Progressive Ideology and Minority Politics during the New Deal," University of Oregon, 1961.

Relevant memoirs include Alben Barkley, "*That Reminds Me*, (Doubleday, 1954); James A. Farley, *Jim Farley's Story* (McGraw-Hill, 1948); Herbert Hoover, *Memoirs*, three volumes (Macmillan, 1951–52); Harold Ickes, *The Secret Diary of Harold L. Ickes*, three volumes (Simon and Schuster, 1953–54); Robert L La Follette, *La Follette's Autobiography*, (Wisconsin, 1911); David E. Lilienthal, *The Journals of David E. Lilienthal*, volume one (Harper and Row, 1964); Henry Cabot Lodge, *The Senate and the League of Nations* (Scribners, 1925); Henry Cabot Lodge Jr., *The Storm Has Many Eyes* (Norton, 1973); Joseph W. Martin, as told to Robert J. Donovan, *My First Fifty Years in Politics* (McGraw-Hill, 1960); George W. Norris, *Fighting Liberal* (Macmillan, 1945); Carl Smith;, *Carl Smith in Washington* (Binford and Mort, 1940); Arthur H. Vandenberg Jr., *The Private Papers of Senator Vandenberg* (Houghton Mifflin, 1952); and John Morton Blum, editor, *The Price of Vision: The Diary of Henry A. Wallace* (Houghton Mifflin, 1973).

Of the scores of biographies of McNary's contemporaries the following studies provided valuable information: John A. Garraty, *Henry Cabot Lodge* (Knopf, 1953); Marian C. McKenna, *Borah* (Michigan, 1961); Harry Barnard, *Independent Man: The Life of Senator James Couzens* (Scribners, 1958): Belle Case La Follette and Fola La Follette, *Robert M. La Follette*, two volumes, (Macmillan, 1953); Joseph Hutmacher, *Robert Wagner and the Rise of Urban Liberalism* (Atheneum, 1968); Richard Lowitt, *George W. Norris*, three volumes (Syracuse, Illinois, 1963–1978); James Patterson, *Mr. Republican: A Biography of Robert A. Taft*, (Houghton Mifflin, 1972); C. David Tompkins, *Senator Arthur Vandenberg: The Evolution of a Modern Republican* (Michigan State, 1970); Gilbert Fite, *George N. Peek and the Fight for Farm Parity* (Oklahoma, 1954); Donald L. Winters, *Henry Cantwell Wallace as Secretary of Agriculture* (Illinois, 1970); and Edward L. Schapsmier and Frederick H. Schapsmier, *Henry A. Wallace of Iowa: The Agrarian Years* (Iowa State, 1968), Richard Norton Smith, *Thomas E. Dewey and His Times* (Simon and Schuster, 1982), and Steve Neal, *Dark Horse: A Biography of Wendell Willkie* (Doubleday, 1984).

For background on the administrations that McNary worked with, there is a wealth of presidential literature. I profited most from these works: Arthur Link, *Wilson*, five volumes (Princeton, 1947–1965); Thomas A. Bailey, *Woodrow Wilson and the Great Betrayal* (Macmillan, 1945); Robert K. Murray, *The Harding Era* (Minnesota, 1969); John D. Hicks, *Republican Ascendancy: 1921–1933* (Harper and Row, 1960); Donald McCoy, *Calvin Coolidge: The Quiet President* (Macmillan, 1967); Joan Hoff Wilson, *Herbert Hoover: Forgotten Progressive* (Little, Brown, 1975); Albert U. Romasco, *The Poverty of Abundance: Hoover, the Nation, the Depression* (Oxford, 1965); Harris G. Warren, *Herbert Hoover and the Great Depression* (Oxford, 1959); James MacGregor Burns, *Roosevelt: The Lion and The Fox* (Harcourt, 1956), and *Roosevelt: Soldier of Freedom* (Harcourt, 1970); William E. Leuchtenberg, *Franklin D. Roosevelt and the New Deal* (Harper and Row, 1963); Arthur M. Schlesinger, *The Age of Roosevelt*, three volumes (Houghton Mifflin, 1956–60); and Frank Freidel, *Franklin D. Roosevelt* four volumes (Little Brown, 1952–73).

Unhappily there is not much literature on Oregon politics of this period.

Robert E. Burton's *Democrats of Oregon: The Pattern of Minority Politics* (Oregon, 1970) is a competent study. Gordon B. Dodds' *Oregon: A History* (Norton, 1977) contains a perceptive sketch of McNary. Earl Pomeroy's *The Pacific Slope* (Knopf, 1965) is a first-rate treatment of the Far West, including McNary's Oregon. Richard L. Neuberger's *Our Promised Land* (Macmillan, 1938) is a collection of that gifted writer's Pacific Northwest writings with special attention to the region's politics including firsthand observations on Senator McNary.

INDEX

[Italicized page numbers refer to illustrations]

Colophon

THE TYPEFACE used in *McNary of Oregon* is Baskerville, a time-honored face originally created by John Baskerville of Birmingham, England. Baskerville, a man of wide-ranging interests, became Cambridge University's printer in 1758 after working as a stone carver, writing master and japanned goods manufacturer. In 1766 he designed the original cutting of Baskerville, often called the first of the transitional romans due to its greater differentiation of thick and thin strokes and the nearly horizontal serifs on the lower case letters. Text and display typography was set by G & S Typesetters Inc. of Austin, Texas.

This volume was printed by Salem Offset Service, Inc. of Salem, Oregon, the home town of both the author, Steve Neal, and the subject of this biography, Charles McNary. *McNary of Oregon* is printed on 6olb. Warren Olde Style, an acid-free paper conforming to national permanent paper standards. Binding was provided by Lincoln & Allen Company of Portland, Oregon. This volume was designed and produced by Western Imprints, The Press of the Oregon Historical Society.